POSTCOLONIAL BERGSON

SOULEYMANE BACHIR DIAGNE

Translated by Lindsay Turner

Fordham University Press gratefully acknowledges financial assistance and support provided for the publication of this book by Columbia University.

Copyright © 2019 Fordham University Press

All rights reserved. No part of this publication may be reproduced, stored in a retrieval system, or transmitted in any form or by any means—electronic, mechanical, photocopy, recording, or any other—except for brief quotations in printed reviews, without the prior permission of the publisher.

This book was first published in French as *Bergson postcolonial: L'élan vital dans la pensée de Léopold Sédar Senghor et de Mohamed Iqbal*, by Souleymane Bachir Diagne © 2011 CNRS Éditions, Paris.

Cet ouvrage a bénéficié du soutien des Programmes d'aide à la publication de l'Institut Français.

This work, published as part of a program of aid for publication, received support from the Institut Français.

Fordham University Press has no responsibility for the persistence or accuracy of URLs for external or third-party internet websites referred to in this publication and does not guarantee that any content on such websites is, or will remain, accurate or appropriate.

Fordham University Press also publishes its books in a variety of electronic formats. Some content that appears in print may not be available in electronic books.

Visit us online at www.fordhampress.com.

Library of Congress Cataloging-in-Publication Data

Names: Diagne, Souleymane Bachir, author. | Turner, Lindsay, translator.
Title: Postcolonial Bergson / Souleymane Bachir Diagne ; translated by Lindsay Turner.
Other titles: Bergson postcolonial. English
Description: New York : Fordham University Press, 2020. | Includes bibliographical references and index. | Summary: "At a moment of renewed interest in Bergson's philosophy, this book, by a major figure in both French and African philosophy, gives an expanded idea of the political ramifications of Bergson's thought in a postcolonial context"—Provided by publisher.
Identifiers: LCCN 2019028522 | ISBN 9780823285839 (hardback) | ISBN 9780823285822 (paperback) | ISBN 9780823285846 (epub)
Subjects: LCSH: Iqbal, Muhammad, Sir, 1877–1938—Philosophy. | Senghor, Léopold Sédar, 1906–2001—Philosophy. | Bergson, Henri, 1859–1941—Influence. | Decolonization. | Postcolonialism.
Classification: LCC B2430.B43 D52413 2020 | DDC 194—dc23
LC record available at https://lccn.loc.gov/2019028522

21 20 19 5 4 3 2 1
First edition

CONTENTS

FOREWORD: LOCATING THE POSTCOLONIAL IDEA

JOHN E. DRABINSKI

> Henri Bergson teaches us how to read philosophers: we must begin by taking a step back from their thought in order to return to its sources, weigh the influences that nurtured it and pinpoint the ideas of which the doctrine is a synthesis. But the real fruit of this effort, Bergson indicates, is reaped at the point where we discover the initial intuition of which the doctrine is an unfolding.
>
> —SOULEYMANE BACHIR DIAGNE, *AFRICAN ART AS PHILOSOPHY*

Who is Bergson to the postcolonial moment?

This is no small question. In it, we find some of the most perplexing enigmas of thinking the postcolonial.

What is a text? What is a text in relation to the author? What is the text in relation to the historical moment? And the author to the historical moment, folded back into the relation to the text? These are all questions that inhere in any critical reading practice, to be sure, especially now that we are a number of decades past the emergence of historicism as a form of inquiry and interpretation. A text does not float outside of time and therefore carries with it so many elements of history and memory. History and memory bear on a text in ways that sustain, enable, and extend the meaning of arguments and descriptions. This is what it means to encounter a text inside a tradition. When we encounter a text inside a tradition, presuming the notion of tradition to be stable and productive (no small assumption), intertextuality is everything; references internal and external to the particular text bring a writerly endeavor to life and we who interpret for a living, professional Hermes figures, draw deeply on such references as referrals and deferrals both.

But the postcolonial moment is something very different. The postcolonial text is always fraught and tense. Conflicted over its own temporality. Puzzling over the fecundity of the past and also the pitfalls of the backward glance at every turn. Critical eyes more appropriately fixed on what the future might mean when it comes. Temporality is conflicted because the text emerges in time, carrying with it all the stains and limits of the past, shrouded sometimes in the awfulness of historical atrocity, animated in other cases by the parochialism or small world vision of its author and the author's epoch. At the same time, *in* the same time, the texts bears a productive past. Sometimes in traces and fragments, in other times as a suppressed vital force waiting on the margins for space within which to operate, and always, in the postcolonial moment, as a kind of volcanic force. From beneath the surface, an antithesis to the colonial model and its domination. Between these two times, the time of domination and the time of a past difference now become resistance, the future emerges as a project for thinking.

Bergson's work is such an interesting site for reflection. The vitalist movement, of which he was such an important member, faded quickly from center stage in France and Europe following the First World War, overtaken in the years leading up to and then after the Second World War by existentialism and phenomenology. But Bergson remained the influential figure of that moment, registering a deep mark on the work of Jean-Paul Sartre, Maurice Merleau-Ponty, Gilles Deleuze, Emmanuel Lévinas, and many others. That legacy tells a fairly straightforward story. Influenced by his insistence on time, temporality, and the moment, then infused with emerging phenomenological and existential methodologies coming out of Germany, French philosophy transformed Bergsonian thinking while also giving structural rigor and depth to his most foundational claims.

In the postcolony? This is a more complicated story. Donna Jones's excellent critical genealogy of vitalist thought in the Negritude movement, the 2010 book *The Racial Discourses of Life Philosophy*, draws out this complicated relation of influence and transformation, identifying in clear terms how Bergson's thought, through both his own articulations and its uses and abuses by colonial thinkers, operated as a legitimizing infrastructure of racial prejudice and colonial domination at the level of politics, culture, and intellectual production. At the same time, however, Bergson's work spread its influence in the colonies, taking up important roles in the works of some of the most important anticolonial thinkers of the era. In particular, Léopold Senghor, to whom so many of the pages in *Postcolonial Bergson* are dedicated. Indeed, Senghor's conception of Negritude is nearly inseparable from an engagement with Bergson's thought, at the level of both tone and frame and the methods by which one rigorously interrogates the Africanness at the heart of Senghor's thinking. A half-caste thought, as he puts it, but also a robust, unmediated Africanness rooted in long-standing traditions of speech, gesture, art, and dance. Bergson's work gets Senghor inside Africanness. We can see immediately how *this* postcolonial thought is fraught. What does it mean to take a white Western thinker to bear on African thinking? This is an anxious sort of moment for many folks working in postcolonial theory and cultural politics. For Senghor, however, it was always a productive relation. As it was for Muhammad Iqbal, a thinker of reconstruction after the colony. And so many others across the anglo- and francophone worlds of the Global South.

What demands does such a dynamic place on our reading? And how do those demands shift our understanding of important, even radical, postcolonial theorizing at the moment of emancipation and liberation?

Readers of the tradition of Negritude, Black Atlantic theory, and francophone African philosophy know Souleymane Bachir Diagne's work well. One of the most important thinkers of his generation, Diagne's writing brings a quiet intensity to matters of logic, historical experience, and the project of theorizing thinking itself in the wake of colonial domination, always between worlds of language and religion. He is such a singular and intriguing figure, mixing unexpected fields in his writing, first, on Boolean logic in *Boole, 1815–1864: L'oiseau de nuit en plein jour*, then turning systematic thinking and reflection toward questions of religion (Islam in particular, through an engagement with the work of Iqbal) and art in thinking the postcolonial in the 2016 book *The Ink of the Scholars*, among others.

The postcolonial is no simple story in Diagne's work. In fact, he eschews (or perhaps better *complicates* and *contests*) so many of the easy distinctions that animate contemporary work on race, nation, and philosophy. Conventional divisions that implicitly (or explicitly) draw on racial essentialisms get little traction in Diagne's work, not out of a supervening sense of humanism or common humanity but out of two key features of his thinking: curiosity and intuition. Curiosity inheres in Diagne's incredible literacy; his capacity to evoke, say, writerly and interpretative practices in Timbuktu and also enigmas of Cartesian mathematical logic is all but unprecedented in contemporary thought. It is really remarkable and on display in *Postcolonial Bergson* at every turn. And the commitment to intuition, the most Bergsonian of insights, draws curiosity and logical rigor back to the life sources of thought itself. Our claims are measured by their link to intuitive life, to our embodied presence to the world and its subjection to time, which opens a collage of thinkers and modes of thought to the perplexing questions of postcolonial theory and cultural practice. This shift from an ethnoracial essentialism toward the open curiosity of thinking *from* and *through* Bergsonian notions of intuition makes all the difference in the world—and all the world's differences are therein made philosophical, intriguing, transformative, and significant. I am thinking here of the introductory remarks to *The Ink of the Scholars* in which Diagne recalls a question directed to him by Paulin Hountondji after a presentation on Descartes, Boole, Leibniz, and algebraic logic. Hountondji asks, in Diagne's recollection: "In your university, in Dakar, or anywhere else in Africa, would you have treated this same conference topic in the same way?" What does this question mean? What is at stake in asking it and then in answering it? Diagne responds:

> The audience understood it as an accusation: I had "forgotten" to speak of Descartes, the respondent seemed to say, from my position as an *African* philosopher, from my *difference*, and on the contrary had installed myself comfortably *among* Descartes, Leibniz, and Boole, at the heart of a history of philosophy and mathematics tacitly agreed upon as *ours*, all of us, since those in the amphitheatre shared the *same identity* as these philosophers.[1]

What the respondents assume is that "Descartes from an African perspective," as Diagne puts it, is an *imperative* and political-cultural inevitability. The failure to do so creates a kind of cultural-intellectual crisis. (Hountondji, of course, was asking something very different.) Why is it imperative? Why would we expect such a form of engagement? Are other engagements—namely, the sort Diagne had given in the preceding talk and across so much of his work—derivative, estranged, or irresponsible? Again, it returns us to the postcolonial moment and its texts. To what time is that text subjected? And to what time is the reader-interpreter subjected? What reading emerges from the time of encounter in the postcolonial?

In many ways, this moment, which, while anecdotal, describes the complexity of Diagne's work in a flash, hearkens back to the work of one of his key philosophical sources: Léopold Senghor. Senghor's vision of

Negritude was utterly singular and is in many ways best understood in contrast to the same-but-different project articulated by his comrade Aimé Césaire. Césaire famously invoked the term *Negritude* in his epic poem *Notebook of a Return to the Native Land* in reference to the Haitian Revolution, initiating a Black Atlantic intellectual and political movement with appeal to the historic moment in which Negritude, an unapologetic and potent sense of Blackness, stood up as resistance and self-emancipation to French enslavers. The revolution teaches us an important lesson, according to Césaire: Whatever the punishing history of anti-Blackness, from the Middle Passage to enslavement and the disastrous machine of the plantation, there remains a sense of Blackness that resists abjection. Colonialism *aimed* at being a total project but could not kill off the revolutionary and transformative potential of Blackness as a form of vitality and life philosophy. Anti-Blackness buries this potential, to be sure, but does not eliminate it. Colonialism is catastrophic violence, but it is not total. What is buried contains within itself the possibility of new (or renewed) life. Thus, across *Notebook* Césaire evokes the volcano and the volcanic, the buried possibility of explosion that both destroys the present and creates the new. In a New World context, this is the resonance of Negritude as a cultural and racial project. Césaire's Negritude is constructed in the ruins of life and history, full of promise amid fragments and fragmentation.

Senghor's conception of Negritude is so very different, in large part because he is responding to a different geography of crisis. The archipelago, Césaire's space of crisis, is figuratively what history and memory had made of Afro-Caribbean subjectivity and cultural life: a collection of fragments in need of visions of unity. Césaire, Léon Damas, and others stepped into this crisis with a vision of civilizational unity that promised to transform cultural production and the world of ideas.[2] But Senghor's task was very different. The colonial situation in Senegal, and indeed across the continent of Africa, bequeathed a very different history and therefore a very different set of decolonial tasks. Rather than a crisis of sources and resources in fragments, Senghor confronts a new reality of extant and future sources. The extant sources turn to African artistic and literary traditions, which, on Senghor's treatment, are by and large embedded in oral traditions and symbolic living plastic forms. Senghor's contribution to thinking radically about postcolonial art and culture lies in his uncompromised assessment of these traditions—namely, that the literary, artistic, and cultural forms expressed therein represent profound insights and rich, powerful interrogations of humanity. At the same time, these traditions, if left in the cast of the past, are not compatible with modern—by which Senghor means remnants of the colonial, folded into a transforming postcolonial vision—systems of education. Translation becomes necessary.

Translation as transformation, to be sure, but also as the work of conservation in the interest of a postcolonial future. Senghor writes:

> For Africa, there is the same problem to-day, especially in the study of French literature. I would like to see in secondary schools every exercise and every essay a continual confrontation and yet at the same time a continual exchange of opinions between Europe and Africa. . . . As in France teaching of French goes with the teaching of the classical languages, it would be good in African secondary schools to make it compulsory to study a vernacular language with French.[3]

There is a lot to be said about this passage, but what strikes me reading it over seven decades after its composition is Senghor's articulation of something akin to hybridity. Hybridity, here, not as compromise but as confrontation and exploration of difference. Vernacular language is no mere prop, nor is it, as it would be for Ngũgĩ wa Thiong'o some forty years later in *Decolonising the Mind*, a straightforward revolutionary act. Rather, Senghor imagines the postcolonial as a space of participation, critical engagement, and dialectical extension of what we *had known* to be a historical and deeply philosophical study of the human person. Again, from the "Education" essay, Senghor writes:

> We have heard for decades about the "modern humanities." Why should there not be "African hu-

> manities"? Every language, which means every civilization, can provide material for the humanities, because *every civilization is the expression, with its own peculiar emphasis, of certain characteristics of humanity.* How can an African élite play its part in bringing about a renaissance of African civilization out of the ferment caused by French contact if they start off knowing nothing about that civilization? And where can a more authentic expression of that civilization be found than in vernacular languages and literature?[4]

Language is inseparable from civilization. This is something Frantz Fanon understood when he wrote in the opening pages of *Black Skin, White Masks* that to speak a language is to bear the weight of its civilization. For Fanon, this is the condition of colonial alienation. For Senghor, it is also (or rather) the imperative to teach the full expressive range of vernacular languages. These languages in writerly translation are deployed not toward a nationalist end but toward the final end of understanding humanity in the widest, deepest sense.

Senghor's humanism comes to the fore here and a version of this humanism animates so much of Diagne's work on Bergson in a postcolonial context. Humanism, for Senghor, is nothing like the European abstraction of the person, consciousness, or some such variation. Rather, humanism is infused with the racial and geographic meaning of subjectivity, a meaning derived from a "spirit of African civilization" that "finds its incarnation in the most everyday reality."[5] Everyday reality is temporal and ecstatic, reaching into the past and projecting into the future—the long duration of the instant, really, showing the influence of Bergsonian thought. And so Senghor writes in "Towards a New African-Inspired Humanism":

> The problem which we, Africans in 1959, are set is how to integrate African values into the world of 1959. It is not a case of reviving the past so as to live on in an African museum. It is a case of animating this world, here and now, with the values that come from our past.[6]

Just as with the matter of language, the imperative to set the vernacular alongside French is an expansive and integrative project. An expansive and integrative project dedicated to the exploration of humanity in its fullest sense, a sense limited, historically, by the political exclusion of Black voices and cultural formations. The postcolonial on this model is nothing like a nationalist project, and very different than the volcanic sense of Negritude in Césaire, but rather something more like W. E. B. Du Bois's vision of the world stage of cultural production and display in his early essay "The Conservation of Races." In Diagne's hands, the expansion of African values into life, beyond the museum, takes on a more robustly complicated Africa, composed of intersections of religion, aesthetic history, language, politics, and the vicissitudes of influence across the continent.

What are we to make of this expansive and integrative project? What does it mean that Senghor eschews the cultural nationalism of so many postcolonial theorists as well as distances himself from an obsessive appeal to the new in thinking a future after colonialism?

These are difficult questions in Senghor and are also at work in Diagne's own prefatory remarks in *The Ink of the Scholars* on the nature of open, curious inquiry. Inquiry draws on a multitude of sources with unpredictable sites of intersection while also and firstly being attuned to the uniqueness of African intellectual traditions. Sites of intersection are answerable to intuition rather than nationalist notions of consciousness and so are matters of assimilating modes of inquiry in the best, most productive sense of the term. It is worth recalling here an early work of Senghor's, a short piece from 1945 entitled "Association and Assimilation." In this piece, Senghor explores some of the political questions of association through federation. Those questions are also about relations between civilizations and cultural production. He writes:

> For the colonies there is the problem of assimilating the spirit of French civilization. It must be an active and judicious assimilation, fertilizing the indigenous civilizations, bringing them out of their stagnation, re-creating them out of their decadence. It must be *an assimilation that leaves room for association.*[7]

I find this passage and companion sentiments across Senghor's early work provocative in the best sense, a sense that Diagne puts to such good work in *Postcolonial Bergson*. It is a remark that recalls, if we can throw these remarks forward, a comment made by Senghor at the 1956 Paris Congrés that Africans "are objectively half-castes."[8] Senghor's notion of the half-caste, however, is neither a compromised nor a melancholic hybridity. Rather, and he makes this clear elsewhere, the assimilation of a cultural *other* is a "moral and intellectual cross-fertilization, a spiritual graft" that is "an assimilation by the African himself."[9] Against the anxieties of ethnoracial nationalism, Senghor asserts the integrity of the African tradition(s). They have nothing to fear from contact, having been restored, in and after Negritude, to their proper place on the world stage.

This returns us, with a history of theorizing the postcolonial outside the ethnoracial nationalism that surrounds so much thinking, to Diagne's important work in *Postcolonial Bergson* and how it continues his long meditation on the place of Bergsonian thinking in the contemporary moment. Diagne's is the work of sympathetic critical genealogy, taking on the notion of élan vital as a crucial and important part of thinking through Senghor's and Iqbal's work rather than turning a skeptical gaze toward their appropriation of the concept. For me, this is a key shift for a number of reasons. First, it is hermeneutically responsible, taking the integrity of the text as a given and a good. Bergson is Diagne's resource here, as the epigraph above from *African Art as Philosophy* demonstrates. What happens when you trace a thought to its sources and read that source of sources with sympathy, generosity, and interpretative rigor? You get the intuition of a doctrine. Intuitive sources, that is, that are embedded in the most productive of visions of a philosophical humanism: the dignity of thought, the intensity of vital sources of being and relation, and the unfolding of doctrines that issue *from* that wellspring of thinking and thought. Second, it places the intensity of life—in its variety, yes, but also in its foundation in intuition and time—at the center of philosophical inquiry. Engagement with Bergson does not estrange. Such engagement expands and integrates. Philosophy as vital practice. And so, third, it displays the force of a thinking that refuses to see subaltern or emergent critical traditions as fatally vulnerable to contact with the colonial other. Bergson was, in some measure, part of that colonial other, an other whose concrete political and cultural reality in the Global South meant suffering, exploitation, and decimation of all aspects of life—including the seriousness of existing, historical philosophical traditions. Assimilation, however, is a creative act. It draws on intuition. It makes influence its own. Assimilation by the African himself. Therein lies the force of thinking in relation, from multiple sources, toward a sense of the human and its creative evolution.

Once one is committed to intuition as a source-point for philosophical thought and doctrine, and complex intersections of histories bear *productively* on the postcolonial text, so much is revealed. Fidelity to fecund possibilities in the case of Bergson, for sure, but also the different temporalities of the African text within Africa. Diagne's long engagement with art as a form of philosophical thinking opens up the question of medium in an African philosophical context. That is such an enormous contribution to philosophical thinking, one made possible, again, in the intersection of historical African aesthetico-theoretical practices with a philosophy rooted in intuition. It is also the intertwining of intuition, oral practices, and the complicated history of writing. Senghor understood this, as noted above; part of creating a postcolonial education system lies in responsible conversion of oral traditions into writing for the sake of classroom instruction and continuity across generations. Cultural reproduction takes place in this conversion. But Diagne, in a fantastic essay on Timbuktu and West African philosophy from 2008, points out that the conversion to writing was already a practice in Islamic Africa, in particular in the tradition of *ajami* literature—"literature using Arabic script in a non-Arabic language."[10] No tradition is pure. Everything is a form of translation, at some level. That is not a confession of compromise but instead an honest reckoning with the vicissitudes of history, of sites of exchange under conditions of curious contact as well as domination and subordination and its companion resistances. I do not think we can call this cosmopolitanism. That is too ethereal. Rather, it is (sometimes painful, sometimes pleasurable) concrete testimony to the persistence of philosophical thinking and its careful, critical work across cultural and political contact, amid the ruins and also in the libraries and amphitheaters of the world. Real philosophical work *beyond* the limits of ethnoracial nationalism goes to all of these sites, measured by intuition, subjected to time as a productive surge in thought and thinking.

Diagne has long since done this sort of work. It is his challenge to us and also his gift. The challenge lies in our own critical practices and how, for so many, the appeal of absolute difference is so real and enduring. Diagne's postcolonial Bergson, his intuitive Senghor and Iqbal, asks something more of us. We are challenged to think at sites of exchange and intuition, to draw ourselves close to the initiation point(s) that make doctrines and facilitate their unfolding. As readers, we are active participants, not distant spectators. Philosophical reading as a kind of immersive experience.

The gift is something that comes from immersion and is made possible by it. Diagne's gift is a text like *Postcolonial Bergson*, a model of rigor and seriousness but also an occasion of real interpretive playfulness and innovation. This book is full of risks in the very same moment that it displays, at every turn, fidelity to texts and their genealogies. How to read philosophers? Return to sources. There are many.

INTRODUCTION

The fifth volume of the journal *Annales Bergsoniennes* was devoted to the theme of "Bergson and Politics."[1] The purpose of this volume, edited by Frédéric Worms, was to explore a subject not often discussed in studies of the philosopher's thought. In his preface, Vincent Peillon lamented the insufficient attention previously given to Henri Bergson's political philosophy. According to Peillon, the cause of this negligence was the received idea that before theorizations of "engagement" by public thinkers such as Sartre and Camus, and by certain Marxist intellectuals, French philosophy—especially Bergson's—treated purely metaphysical themes, themes that had no material purchase or effect on the political course of world events. Such an a priori, Peillon wrote, ignored the actual engagements of prewar philosophers, which had often involved real diplomatic action through which their philosophical thought was reflected and became visible.

Bergson, as Peillon underscored, led significant diplomatic action. Above all, he also laid the philosophical foundation for the notion of an "open society" as a society always in the process of opening still more for the new, the stranger, the migrant. In this way, his thought exercised a "progressive political influence" that deserves attention. This is even more the case when his ideas—ideas that might seem purely metaphysical, such as élan vital, duration, or intuition—turn out to have had political ramifications, beginning with their reception by thinkers *who had read Bergson*. In a tremendously accurate phrase, Peillon calls this "Bergsonian philosophy's action at a distance."

Such "action at a distance" is the subject of this book. Specifically, *Postcolonial Bergson* studies the way this action at a distance occurs in the encounter between the work of the French philosopher and the work of two thinkers from the colonial world: Muhammad Iqbal (1877–1938), from India, and Léopold Sédar Senghor (1906–2001), from Senegal.

Before turning to these two writers, I want first to lay out more broadly the action of Bergsonian thought in the colonies generally, or the impact it had on intellectuals from what today we call the Global South. To do this, I will first consider the reception, in the colonized world, of Bergson's lecture to the Academy of Moral and Political Sciences on December 12, 1914.

Several months earlier, on July 28, 1914, Austria-Hungary had declared war on Serbia, setting off the chain of events that culminated in the First World War. Bergson's subject for the academy's annual public session could not have been anything other than the war and its horrors. And, in fact, he began by stating that circumstances required that his speech be a "cry of horror and of indignation" in the face of "the crimes methodically committed by Germany: arson, pillage, destruction of monuments, massacre of women and children, violation of all the laws of war."[2] But beyond expressing indignation, there remained the necessity of "drawing out the meaning of this war," understanding it "philosophically," so to speak. And indeed, the speech quickly became a reflection on the "mechanical" and the "living," notions at the heart of Bergson's philosophy, independent of any particular circumstances.

German aggression, Bergson said, was only the continuation of the violent manner in which Prussia chose to bring about German unification: through mechanical or artificial means and not by supporting and directing "the natural effort of life." Thus, rather than accompanying what Bergson called "the ordinary work of life," the force that could have brought together the German nations and then linked them organically into an expanded, open whole, Prussia had launched a mechanical, technical process that had forced the artificial unification of parties that remained external to each other. It is this process of mechanical addition that would snowball into the terrible war Germany waged on civilization. Its victory would be the triumph of materialism and of technology against the force of life. Thus, we see that in Bergson's 1914 speech, the opposition between élan vital and technological power appeared as the expression of the most pressing political question that could exist: war or peace.

In April of 1916, a summary of Bergson's lecture was published in Arabic by the journal *Al-Muqtataf* in Cairo. This monthly scientific review had been founded in Beirut in 1876 and then moved to Cairo in 1885. As its name suggested, it was a "digest" in which intellectuals from Egypt, Libya, Iraq, Syria, and Yemen—as well as Iran, India, and China—were able to learn of and discuss the latest scientific and technological advances, as well as the major philosophical questions of the day. The journal remained active until 1952.[3] The Arabic translation of the main points of Bergson's speech led to a rich discussion around the question of materialism as a philosophy that carried within itself the possibility of war, as opposed to the civilizing force of the spirit.

Such discussion was the prolongation of a conversation that had continued since the journal's founding, issue after issue and year after year, about Darwinism and its implications. In fact, the scientific periodical was, in the words of Marwa Elshakry, "one of the most important sources of information about Darwin"[4] and "was to play a crucially important role in the popularization of Darwin's ideas."[5] The discussion of Darwinism in its pages had turned very quickly into a discussion of evolutionary thought and of materialism in general.

Describing the way Bergson's speech was inscribed into the philosophical and political debate over materialism, Elshakry writes:

> In April 1916, *Al-Muqtataf* published a summary of the speech Henri Bergson had delivered in the first winter of the war in which he had attributed German aggression to materialism itself. Sarruf had already made a similar argument to Shumayyil. The war was the outcome of materialism, Sarruf argued, and he advised Shumayyil to read Bergson's speech. How could Shumayyil now deny the importance of a divine force in securing a cosmic order and overcoming the pursuit of individual self interest? "What would prevent a man from killing anybody who hinders his interests," Sarruf wrote to Shumayyil, "exactly as he kills lions, wolves, and flies? Why should not a man from Paris or Berlin then kill blacks who prevent him from hunting in Africa? Is not the deterrent that keeps strong people from having a free hand with weak people a moral and not a materialist one?"[6]

As reported by Elshakry, this discussion contains important lessons about the way Bergson intervenes in the debate between these Arab intellectuals, Shibli Shumayyil (1850–1917) and Yaqub Sarruf (1852–1927). Sarruf, along with his Lebanese countryman Faris Nimr (1856–1951), was the founder of *Al-Muqtataf.* Both men were passionate about science and devoted to the idea that it constituted a force for social evolution. Shumayyil, who was their classmate at the Syrian Protestant College (which would become the American University of Beirut in 1920), was a doctor, famous in the modern intellectual history of the Arab world for having been an avowed materialist, a champion of the theory of spontaneous generation, and a major figure supporting the idea of Darwinian evolution. The debate described by Elshakry took place in Egypt, where Sarruf and Shumayyil (as well as Nimr) lived.

The first lesson to take from this exchange is that the question of morality is at the heart of the discussion of the Darwinian face of materialism. We see how this is formulated in Sarruf's statement, in his declaration that if matter is itself its own principle, then there is no moral brake forbidding the thought that everything is permitted in the "struggle for life" to which Darwinism was often reduced in the discussions. Materialism would prove the strongest right, thus giving violence free reign.

A second lesson is that this debate takes place against the background of colonialism, even if this is not explicitly mentioned. Is colonialism not an incarnation of that same "materialist" aggression perpetrated by Germany, with that country presenting to the European colonial powers at war with it a face in which they should recognize themselves? The power to kill with impunity the Blacks who oppose my desire to kill all the wild animals I want in Africa—is this not the crime "methodically committed" by the mechanical against the living, of which Bergson speaks?

We might remember that *L'Énergie spirituelle* (published in English as *Mind-Energy*) is the title of the work by Bergson that appeared immediately after the war, in 1919, which brought together the author's "essays and lectures." The first chapter of this work, titled "Life and Consciousness" and originally Bergson's Huxley Lecture of May 24, 1911, at the University of Birmingham, dwells at length on the meaning of evolution, which the French philosopher never considered only to imply materialism. On the contrary, Bergson insists on the fact that evolution shows that there is "visibly . . . a force at work," an "effort" [*force spirituelle*] that for him is the ability to "draw out from the self more than it had already."[7] Above all, he writes, at its heart lies morality: It demonstrates that the "vital movement pursues its way without hindrance, thrusting through the work of art, the human body, which it has created on its way, the *creative current of the moral life*."[8]

When Sarruf thus sends Shumayyil back to a reading of Bergson's speech on the meaning of the war, this invitation to read the French philosopher—and this is a third and final lesson to be taken from the discussion—can be understood more generally, beyond the particular context of this debate, as a call to the force of the spirit, to *énergie spirituelle*, against the violence of materialism, which is also the violence of a mechanical colonialism. Spiritual energy as a force of progress and emancipation, as well as a moral force to be opposed to alienations and material dominance: Here, in a word, is what constitutes "the progressive political influence" of the author of *Creative Evolution*. Here is what constitutes Bergsonism's "action at a distance" among the intellectuals of the colonial world, and here is what leads me to speak of a *Postcolonial Bergson*.

In the words of Damian Howard, as "Bergson decoupled the idea of progress from the fashionable worldview of reductionist materialism," he made a "decisive contribution" to the thinking of these intellectual readers of *Al-Muqtataf*, and others, by "making it possible to be at once religious and progressive."[9] Howard illuminates Bergson's "progressive political influence" in his book *Being Human in Islam: The Impact of the Evolutionary Worldview*. He highlights what a number of intellectuals of the Muslim world found in Bergson that contributed to the manner in which they undertook a rethinking of their own philosophical and spiritual traditions and a formulation of a progressive, decolonizing project: the notion of a "developmental ethos" as opposed to "fixed tradition,"[10] of a "creative evolution of society"[11] within a "cosmic, vitalist progressivism."[12]

Very certainly this is true of the Indian Muslim philosopher Muhammad Iqbal, to whom Howard rightly gives an important place in his book. Howard also shows that Bergson's "progressive political influence" on contemporary Muslim thinkers, who develop what he does not hesitate to call a "Bergsonian Islam," still continues. He mentions the Tunisian historian Muhammad Talbi (1921–2017), who volunteered his enthusiasm for Bergsonism and who advocated a "Quranic hermeneutics which stress a 'dynamic and forward-looking' reading of scripture."[13]

Howard also speaks of my own work, representative, he says, of "Bergsonian Islam."[14] Here Howard is referring the introduction to Muhammad Iqbal's thought that I wrote in French in 2001,[15] which was translated into English in 2011 under the title *Islam and Open Society: Fidelity and Movement in the Philosophy of Muhammad Iqbal*.[16] In this book, indeed, I introduce the way in which Iqbal's philosophy finds the language of Bergsonism beautifully fitted to the expression of what he sees as Islam's dynamic cosmology. I will return to this point.

In addition to the study of the encounter between Bergson and Iqbal, I have examined the intellectual meeting of the Senegalese poet and politician Léopold Sédar Senghor with the French philosopher. The book I devoted to Senghor's philosophy of art, and what it owes to Bergson's thought, was published in 2007 in French[17] and then in English in 2011 under the title *African Art as Philosophy: Senghor, Bergson, and the Idea of Negritude*.[18] In this work I analyzed the manner in which the Catholic thinker Senghor has also inscribed his philosophy into Bergsonism's dynamic, evolutionary cosmology. I emphasized the fact that, for Senghor, spiritual energy is especially to be found in art. Thus, first with Iqbal then with Senghor, I sought to shed light on

Bergson's "action" in the books dedicated to these two authors.

What brings Senghor and Iqbal together was not lost on Edgar Faure (1908–1988), a politician, historian, essayist, and member of the French Academy. On March 29, 1984, in his speech welcoming Léopold Sédar Senghor into the French Academy, Faure twice referred, during his praise of the poet-president, to another man of state, also a poet and philosopher: the Indian Muhammad Iqbal. Faure addressed the new "Immortal" by declaring that "the culmination of your research is the goal of totalizing time with space, of uniting two universals and trespassing, in the etymological sense of the word, the dichotomy of their images in the mirror of our imperfect intellection." He then illustrated his point with the following verses:

> Thou hast extended Time, like Space,
> And distinguished Yesterday from To-morrow.
> Our Time which has neither beginning nor end,
> Blossoms from the flower bed of our mind.
> To know its root quickens the living with new life:
> Its being is more splendid than the dawn.
> Life is of Time, and Time is of Life.[19]

"Thus spoke Muhammad Iqbal," the orator added. At the end of his speech, he again cited Iqbal's poetry:

> Appear, O Rider of Destiny!
> Appear, O light of the dark realm of Change!

Silence the noise of the nations.
Imparadise our ears with thy music!
Arise and tune the harp of brotherhood.[20]

Turning back to Senghor, Faure concluded: "Hasn't this apostrophe found [in you] its addressee?"

Edgar Faure perceived what these two men have in common: philosophers, poets, and statesmen who thought the independence of their colonized countries and helped bring it about—even if Iqbal died almost ten years before the separate accessions of India and Pakistan to sovereignty. The community of their thought is real, deeper even than the similarities Faure's comparisons call to mind. It could be called Bergsonism.

Whether in Léopold Sédar Senghor's defense of the values of Negritude or in Muhammad Iqbal's project of the "reconstruction of religious thought in Islam" (the title of his major prose work), at the heart of these projects is Bergson's philosophical thought. The Bergsonian revolution and the main concepts in which it is incarnated—vitalism, time as duration, intuition as *other* approach to the real, expressed particularly in art—thus exercised a considerable influence on the thought of Senghor and Iqbal. This influence is the object of the following four chapters.

How did these two figures of the colonized world come to be Bergsonian? For what reasons, in undertakings as different as Senghor's Negritude and Iqbal's Islamic reformism, did they come to lean on Bergson's thought? First of all, at the moments at which their two philosophies were being developed—the late 1910s to the late 1920s for Iqbal and the 1930s for Senghor—it was practically inevitable that they should be in dialogue with Bergson's philosophy. As Worms explains, this philosophy was given the task of "intervening in life to reform it or to transform it"; it thus became the object of a true "infatuation . . . that spread throughout France and Europe, even beyond, up until the first world war!"[21]

Indeed, "infatuation" describes Senghor's relation to Bergsonism well. To underscore the considerable importance of this thought in the history of philosophy, the Senegalese poet spoke of the "revolution of 1889," the year of publication for Bergson's first work, which was originally his doctoral thesis: *Time and Free Will: An Essay on the Immediate Data of Consciousness* [*Essai sur les données immédiates de la conscience*]. In the case of Iqbal, Iqbal affirms that Bergsonism represents the upwelling of a radical novelty in the history of Western philosophy in its concept of pure time, or duration. He, too, might have spoken of the revolution created by the publication of Bergson's first book in 1889.

In this book, as we know, the philosopher presents his thought as that which has come to correct the error of taking time as "a homogeneous medium" thought only as space (for example, as the interval separating one event from another) while, he says, real *duration*—that is, nonserial time—is "made up of moments internal to one another." Of this duration, we cannot have the type of knowledge produced by our analytic, mechanical intelligence, the one that separates the subject from the object and breaks the latter into its constitutive parts. On the contrary, duration is communicated to us through the vital knowledge we have of it, in the intuition that sets us immediately at the heart of the object, grasped as organic totality.

What Senghor and Iqbal read in the author of *Time and Free Will* was the manner in which he opened new possibilities of thinking outside of a philosophical tradition: a tradition that took a turn, at a certain historical moment, when what had been understood, in intension, as *logos* (which we could take to mean an understanding of the unity of life) was now understood in extension as *ratio* (in other words, an intelligence that detaches its object from itself in order to know it, divides it into parts then mechanically puts them back together—in short, stretches it as space).

Thus, Senghor follows Bergson in undertaking the task of finding a new, comprehensive approach to the real, outside the course of philosophical thought as it had been oriented by Aristotle and outside what culminated in the mechanistic thought of Descartes and scientistic positivism. This nonmechanistic approach appeared to him as the meaning of African art, in which he saw the manifestation of a *vital* knowledge of the real, which he understands as an access to the *subreality* of visible things. He also follows Bergson via his engagement with another Bergsonian, Father Pierre Teilhard de Chardin, extending Bergson's thought into thought of an emergent cosmology, of a cosmogenesis in which life is liberated from the alienations that shackle it. It is from this double perspective—Bergsonian and Teilhardian—that Senghor undertakes a rereading of Marx and proposes a doctrine of what he calls "African socialism."

For Iqbal, too, Bergson provides a way out of the frame in which the philosophical tradition after the pre-Socratics had enclosed philosophy. With Bergson, he was able to find a philosophy of movement in which—in a universe constantly in the process of renewing itself—the human comes about and becomes himself via his creative action, which makes him into God's "collaborator." According to Iqbal, if the introduction of Greek philosophy into the Islamic world constituted an undeniable opening for Muslim thought, it also led to the view of a cosmology fixed once and for all by a divine fiat that then retreated from the world. Such a view constituted a bad translation and a betrayal of the dynamic and continually emergent cosmology of the Quran, in which God is always at work in his creation. Thus, for Iqbal, Bergson's revolution in philosophy helps the reconstruction of Islamic thought, as a reminder that life is innovation and change. The "reminder" was necessary so that Islamic thought could overcome its fear of innovation (always blameworthy as "novelty," according to some) and return, with the dynamic cosmology of the Quran reread through the categories contemporary science has taught us to think, to the true meaning of the continuous "effort of adaptation" to the vital push that is *ijtihad*. Far from confining its meaning into a legal framework, in which *ijtihad* is simply translated as the "effort of interpreting" the cases arising under the light of those that have already been settled, for Iqbal this term is the very principle of movement constitutive of Islam, which Muslim thought today must take up again to escape the petrification that has gripped it since the thirteenth century, and to free itself from the fatalist immobilism to which it is identified, for example, by Leibniz, who coined the concept of *fatum mahometanum*.

When, in his role of chair at the Collège de France, Henry Laurens invited me to give a series of lectures at that institution every Monday for a month, I saw an opportunity to go back to the encounter between Senghor and Iqbal and Bergsonian thought, back to what I had called "Bergson in the colony."[22] These four lectures constitute the chapters of this book.

The first chapter, "Bergsonism in the Thought of Léopold Sédar Senghor," examines the importance for Senghor's philosophy of Negritude of the distinction established by the author of *Creative Evolution* between analytic and intuitive knowledge. Senghor translates this distinction by speaking of a "reason-eye," which operates in separation from its object, and a "reason-embrace," which, on the contrary, realizes a coincidence with its object, becoming one with it. The domain par excellence of this intuitive knowledge—of *e-motion*, a movement by which, following the etymology of the word, the subject goes from separation to *being-with* the object—is art. Intuition is the human aesthetic faculty itself, for it is our capacity to welcome objects as they present themselves to us, cleared of interest in their utility. This faculty is the capacity to grasp the simple movement of life. The artist, says Bergson, is the one who manifests the nature of this immediate grasp that makes it possible to be on the same wavelength as the bare object, stripped of the conventions that are habitually imposed between it and us. In this way, the artist teaches what it means to embrace the movement of life, to become one with it. Thus, wrote Bergson, our relationship with a writer is not a face-off with the words in which he expresses himself. On the contrary, we forget that words are used and instead "the waves of his thought . . . stir us sympathetically"; we enter into "the flow of meaning which runs through the words" in which "two minds which, without intermediary, seem to vibrate directly in unison with one another" thus meet.[23] Senghor echoes this image of meeting in the same undulation when he writes that when we contemplate an art object we receive it in a "rhythmic attitude," which means that we are truly on its wavelength: We *dance* it.

Chapter 2 is titled "Senghor's African Socialism." It is dedicated to the political writings of the Senegalese statesman. Senghor's reading of Marxism owes much to his familiarity with the work of Pierre Teilhard de Chardin, himself strongly influenced by Bergson. First and foremost, like a number of Catholics open to Marxism as demand for social justice, he considered the so-called young Marx as the true Marx: the Marx of the *1844 Manuscripts*, whose language was that of revolt, in the name of ethics, against the "alienated work" that is the hallmark of the capitalist system. Because he took élan vital as the push that leads humans and societies to converge around the realization of what Teilhard de Chardin called a "humanization" or a "socialization of the Earth," Senghor always saw in socialism generally—and in African socialism, in particular—the promise for the human to become *homo artifex*, the creator emancipated from all alienations: colonialism, as well as capitalist exploitation of human work. In thinking socialism and seeking the way to make it a doctrine constituted by and for Africans, the Senegalese philosopher thinks it as the force of life versus the mechanicism of separation: separation of the human from their work, from other humans, from their own humanity.

The third chapter, "Bergson, Iqbal, and the Concept of *Ijtihad*," presents the trajectory of Muhammad Iqbal, who is considered the "founding father of Pakistan" but was first and foremost without question the most important reformist philosopher of Islam. This chapter examines the connections between Bergsonian philosophy of creative evolution and becoming-individual and the Iqbalian aim of a reconstruction and a revivification of Islamic thought, one founded on the notion of the human ego working as *collaborator* with God in its own realization, in "the growing of the personality,"[24] in the action of bringing about the continuously open world of creation.

Chapter 4, "Time and Fatalism: Iqbal on Islamic Fatalism," questions the presentation Leibniz gives of Islamic thought as a philosophy of fatalism he calls *fatum mahometanum*, or *Turkish* (or Islamic) *fatalism*. Here we examine how the German philosopher's analysis is founded on the prejudice that Islam is a doctrine of absolute predestination. Against such bias, which itself presupposes the cosmology of a closed work in which the future is already determined in some sense, Iqbal declares that the Quran's cosmology is that of a continuously emerging universe, open to the creative action of the human. Moreover, he insists that Bergson is the only philosopher to have thought time in itself—which is to say, time as duration. As such, he says, Bergson can in fact help think such a cosmology, particularly by making heard the Prophet of Islam's phrase: "Do not vilify time, for time is God."

I will end this exposition of a "postcolonial" Bergson—even though Bergson himself wrote nothing in particular about colonialism—with a word on the meaning of Bergson's work for us, today, in our post-Bandung world.[25] Against tribalisms and the instinct toward enclosure in which they originate, Bergson's philosophy—especially *The Two Sources of Morality and Religion*, the last work that he published during his life—calls us to raise ourselves to the moral idea of *humanity* that comes to us from philosophical reason, as well as from religion.

As it presents itself—especially with religion—as emotion and generosity, this idea of humanity takes us out of ourselves, out of our ethnonationalist enclosures. In the same spirit, Muhammad Iqbal condemned "the idols of race and tribe," condemning with the same blow the fanaticisms to which these give birth. This is certainly a message our world now needs to hear.

1

BERGSONISM IN THE THOUGHT OF LÉOPOLD SÉDAR SENGHOR

Across the writings of the Senegalese poet Léopold Sédar Senghor, we find the names that make up his literary and intellectual genealogy. These include Arthur Rimbaud, Paul Claudel, and Charles Baudelaire; he explains that despite the connections between his work and Saint-John Perse's, he only discovered the latter late in his career. On the African side are the poets he calls his "Three Graces" or sometimes his "Muses": three female poets from his homeland, inspired composers of *gymnique* songs in honor of Serer wrestlers, Serer being the ethnicity to which Senghor belonged. Philosophers he cites include Pierre Teilhard de Chardin, of course Karl Marx, Jacques Maritain, Gaston Berger, occasionally Friedrich Nietzsche, and always Bergson. Senghor takes every opportunity to remind us that his thought is born out of what he calls the "1889 revolution."

The year 1889 marked the publication of Henri Bergson's doctoral thesis, *Time and Free Will*. Here is Senghor's description of that year's significance for the history of thought and poetic creation: "1889 is . . . an important date in the history of philosophy and literature, as well as the history of art. This is the year of two major works: Henri Bergson's *Time and Free Will* and Paul Claudel's *Tête d'or*, to which I would also add Arthur Rimbaud's *Season in Hell*, which foreshadowed them in 1873, so to speak."[1]

It would be too simple to say that Bergson influenced Senghor's philosophical thought while Rimbaud and Claudel influenced his poetic writing. For Senghor, Bergson represented what we might call the "spirit of 1889" in its totality and brought into being a philosophical truth that was diffused as much in literature as in philosophy, the arts, and even the sciences. Bergson's oeuvre *was* the 1889 revolution.[2]

Let us turn to *Time and Free Will* to examine what in it seemed so revolutionary to Senghor and many others. These "others" include Bergson himself, who was perfectly conscious of the profound rupture that his first book made in the course of the history of philosophy after Aristotle. The revolution of 1889 is not among those movements that become conscious of themselves only after the fact. On the contrary, in the book's concluding lines, after having completed "the analysis of the ideas of duration and voluntary determination"—"the principal object of this work,"[3] as he writes—Bergson affirms that what he has proven has only been possible because he has put an end to the "mistake" of "tak[ing] time to be an homogenous medium" without paying attention to the fact that "that real duration is made up of moments inside one another, and that when it seems to assume the form of a homogeneous whole, it is because it gets expressed in space."[4] This error, which he specifies is also Kant's, is the direction most generally taken by Western thought, led by the Eleatics and their paradoxes about time. These paradoxes, Bergson explains, are born out of a conception that thinks space under the concept of time—or rather, over it, that only thinks time by turning it into spatial extension. For example, time is the distance that separates the moment when I am speaking to you from the one when I will have lunch. We will return in slightly greater depth to this notion of spatialized time, and the problems it entails, when we address the question of Muhammed Iqbal's Bergsonism.

For now, concerning the 1889 revolution's influence on Senghor, let us instead focus on the specific faculty in us that is able to grasp time as interpenetrating moments—in other words, as duration—rather than moments aligned or juxtaposed in a series. To perceive this faculty, Bergson tells us, supposes that, "digging below the surface of contact between the self and external objects, we penetrate into the depths of the organized and living intelligence."[5] More than anything else, this is what composes the "1889 revolution" for Senghor: the illumination, beneath the analytic intelligence—the faculty that understands by analyzing and separating parts external to each other (*partes extra partes*)—of the faculty of vital knowledge, which in a single immediate and instantaneous cognitive gesture can comprehend a composition that is living, not mechanical, and therefore cannot be decomposed. If beneath our conception of time is the understanding of duration—or if, more generally, underneath the apparent immediacy of things (beneath their "bark," as Senghor says) is their reality (for Senghor, "subreality")—this is because beneath the intelligence that analyzes and calculates (in the etymological sense of arranging things as if they were pebbles) there is the intelligence that always synthesizes and that always *comprehends* (here again in the etymological sense).

To recognize the rupture that Bergsonism brings about in the history of Western philosophy, then, as Senghor does, is also to celebrate the fact that this rupture made audible the speech of the comprehending intelligence, first revealing it to itself. Indeed, for Senghor, it is *especially*—although this is not to say exclusively—in the language of the comprehending intelligence that the thoughts and conceptions of the African world are expressed, particularly those that come from works of art. We will return to this. We know what Bergson says about the difficulty of speaking this language, of clearly and distinctly defining a concept such as "duration" in the language of philosophy received from the Aristotelian tradition. We might, though, approach such a concept via metaphor, since the language we ordinarily speak is that of the intelligence-that-separates, for which the idea of time is immediately thought, according to Henri Gouhier, in words and concepts that pertain to the "false immediate" "of useful and useable time, calendar-time and watch-time." The task is therefore to make the language of the intelligence-that-comprehends audible—or, rather, audible *again*. For the Hellenist in Senghor, as well as the Catholic attentive to matters of faith, never fails to remind us that before the analytic turn of thought, toward the *ratio*, there was the reality of what the poet calls the "humid and vibratory" *logos*—which has, so to speak, now dried up.

Ratio on the one hand and *logos* on the other: In two different ways, first in Latin and then in Greek, Senghor translates what is ultimately almost the same thing, presenting two possible approaches to the real. Perhaps more clearly, he also speaks of that difference as between a "reason-eye" and a "reason-embrace." Constant here is the establishment of two ways of knowing: first, an "analytic" cognitive approach, which involves the digging-out of distance between the perceived object and the perceiving subject and which sees the object as the sum of its parts; second, a cognitive approach we will call "synthetic," for symmetry. This approach locates us immediately at the heart of the object, no longer defined in opposition to the subject, at the heart of its "subreality" that is its own rhythm—hence Senghor's frequent play on words in speaking of *thinking* [*penser*] the object as a manner of *dancing* it [*dancer*].

This brings us to a remark about Senghor's philosophy as a philosophy of dance. Since dance is very present in Senghor's theoretical writings, as well as his poetry, it is tempting to see it as simply an African motif. But such an understanding risks missing precisely what Senghor's thought owes to Bergson, from whom Senghor learned to think and formulate the notion of a "corporal cogito," as a movement among the movements of things, a notion that we can also find in contemporary work in neuroscience. Alain Berthoz, for example, shows that the world is not our representation but rather our action, revealing the nature of the brain as a "projector," a "simulator and an emulator" of reality, constructing the world it perceives as a function of the actions it projects.[6]

A name for the other approach Senghor explores, following Bergson, is "emotion," whose etymology (*e-motion*) is always present in the poet's mind when he writes it. This term underscores the primacy of movement in the act of knowing, as opposed to the idea that it is necessary to immobilize in order to grasp. It is important to insist that emotion is not simple feeling but a real cognitive movement, as Jean-Paul Sartre lays out in his *Sketch for a Theory of the Emotions*. Moreover, we know how important Sartre's thought was for Senghor's philosophy, in terms of his analyses of "being-in-the-world" and of emotion, and of course via his influential "preface," *Black Orpheus*, written for Senghor's 1948 poetry anthology that brought together African, Madagascan, and Caribbean poets.

Two consequences follow from Senghor's Bergsonism, understood as this duality between "reason-eye" and "reason-embrace." The first concerns a critique of his thought as ultimately only a reprise of Lucien Lévy-Bruhl's theories of "primitive mentality." The second demonstrates why all of Senghor's thought leads back to a reflection on African art.

What is this supposed Lévy-Bruhlism on Senghor's part, the object of one of the two major critiques of his work? Before quickly returning to this, let us briefly evoke the other critique, which accuses the poet of the mortal sin of essentialism. In this view, Senghor is seen to have presented the meeting—or perhaps the face-off—of cultures as occurring between pure and massive identities in a sort of exaltation of radical difference—in a word, to have simplified the world into black and white. This critique essentially recapitulates an idea already expressed by Sartre in *Black Orpheus*, in which he contended that the movement initiated by Senghor, Césaire, and Damas in the 1930s in Paris corresponded to the figure of the negation of negation, a moment of radical opposition that he even called an "antiracist racism." Such a moment would then ultimately need to transcend itself dialectically into a later moment that would see the advent of a human society without race. For Sartre, the only agent of this advent is the proletariat, which—in the Marxist logic that that structures *Black Orpheus*—is the class that is the bearer of the universal to come.

It is undeniable that Senghor's language is often essentializing. And Sartre is partially correct: In the very principles of the movement that called itself Negritude is what Gayatri Chakravorty Spivak would call a "strategic essentialism"—that is, essentialism as response and resistance. But this language is also continually shadowed by the language of hybridity and fluid identity, and we must be careful not to forget that before he is the poet of Negritude, Senghor is a theorist of *métissage* conceived not as biological accident (what happens to essence, or rather essences, when they meet) but as horizon and norm. Thus, he declares that "each person must be *métis* in their own way."

Returning to the critique that accuses Senghor of Lévy-Bruhlism: Admittedly, the Senegalese poet himself provided grounds for this in one of his first publications. To have written that "emotion is Negro, as reason is Hellenic" [*l'émotion est nègre comme la raision hellène*] purely for the pleasure of crafting an alexandrine! This phrase first appeared in "What the Black Man Contributes," published in 1937, and as it would be "that through which the occasion comes," so to speak, Senghor would find it difficult to shake, the phrase coming almost mechanically to mind whenever Negritude is evoked. Senghor himself would come back to it often, often simultaneously insistent and palinodic.

But let us examine the accusation, which this phrase might seem unfortunately to prove, that Senghor has only reproduced Lucien Lévy-Bruhl's premises, taking the latter's characterization of a prelogical primitive mentality as his own—or, rather, on behalf of African peoples. First, a note on Lévy-Bruhl's method. Philosopher before all else, Lévy-Bruhl set out to establish proof that the study of *ethics and moral science* (this is the title of his 1903 work [*La Morale et la Science des Moeurs*]) can only happen in given singular societies and that there is no such thing as a universal ethics that would apply to "man in general." This conviction leads him to ethnology, a discipline to which he arrives with absolutely no interest in what we call "fieldwork." He is indifferent to what others actually are and has no use for them other than to *know* them as part of a foreign world. Indeed, he might have written the famous opening of Lévi-Strauss's *Tristes Tropiques*: "I hate travelling and explorers." It is not out of interest in others that he turns to ethnology but rather in order to establish their radical alterity, to make them even more other. This is accomplished by setting on one side "our" logic, by which we think within a framework of the principles of identity, contradiction, and excluded middle, and on the other side a prelogic that is so strange to us that it is practically impossible to speak about. All that can be known about it is that it functions according to a "law of participation," which explains its indifference to the principle of contradiction: a sort of "alter-logic" in which it is simultaneously possible to be oneself and to partake of another identity—that of one's totem, for example.

One of the main representatives of this critique of Senghor as Lévy-Bruhlian, endlessly cited, is the Beninese philosopher Stanislas Adotévi, the author of a well-known lampoon entitled *Négritude et négrologues*. This lampoon was written in order to denounce the surreptitious presence of the author of *Primitive Mentality*—even to the point of plagiarism—in Senghor's work. It is unfortunate that Adotévi did not find it necessary simply to read the texts themselves before accusing Senghor of tacitly copying Lévy-Bruhl. For in fact Senghor speaks at length about Lévy-Bruhl, and he clearly indicates the source of the term *participative reason* when he uses it as a synonym for "reason-embrace." Perhaps this is a function of the lampoon genre, but there is worse in this estimation: Adotévi also claims that, in order to hide this imitation of Lévy-Bruhl's thought, Senghor has silently passed over the fact that Lévy-Bruhl repudiated his own thought at the end of his life and—in a palinode published in his posthumous *Carnets* [*Notebooks*]—indicated that humans everywhere share the same logic, founded on the principle of contradiction. Adotévi writes: "Senghor was aware of (but probably rejected) the *Carnets* and the extraordinary honesty of the man who, at the height of official glory, when primitivism was the rage among colonialist and ecstatically reactionary milieus, was not afraid to question everything, thus destroying his life's work."[7]

In terms of Senghor's supposed silence about his relationship to Lévy-Bruhl, we should note the following passage from *Liberté 1*:

> Certainly we have a different temperament, a different soul. But are not these differences in the relationship between elements, rather than in their natures? Beneath these differences, are there not more essential similarities? And especially, is *reason* not *identical* for every man? I do not believe in "prelogical mentality." The soul cannot be prelogical, much less a-logical.[8]

Elsewhere, in the same book apparently too quickly perused by the critic, he writes: "I fear that certain people, even Africans themselves, still believe in Lévy-Bruhl's 'prelogical mentality,' even though the author courageously renounced this theory before his death."[9] My point is not only that we should compare Adotévi's affirmations to the texts that Senghor actually wrote—although certainly this is a useful exercise, since no matter how caustic it is, a lampoon is useless if its assertions do not also ring true. Beyond this, and beyond this individual case, the example demonstrates how often Senghor has been criticized on the basis of what was believed about him, at the expense of any real attention to his writings themselves.

One more note on Lévy-Bruhl's late retraction of his first theses of primitive mentality and prelogic, which was recognized as courageous by Adotévi as well as by

Senghor. We have discussed what led to these theses: the will to establish the philosophical impossibility of "man in general" on the basis of a radical cognitive dualism. Thus, despite a superficial resemblance, an abyss separates this side of Lévy-Bruhl from Bergson, his classmate at the École normale supérieure. This resemblance—again, only superficial—was what led Senghor occasionally to adopt the language of "reason-participation." In fact, Bergson's concept of reasoning-embrace has nothing to do with "participation." However, the Lévy-Bruhl who turns back to cognitive monism at the end of his life has much to do with Bergson's thought.

Relevant here are the pages of *The Two Sources of Morality and Religion* in which Bergson questions the conclusions drawn in the "extremely interesting and instructive books on 'primitive mentality'" by Lévy-Bruhl, in which "M. Lévy-Bruhl emphasizes the indifference of this mentality to proximate or physical causes [and] the fact that it immediately turns to 'mystic causes.'"[10] Considering the examples given by the author of *Primitive Mentality* himself to support his thesis of the prelogic of *others* (i.e., non-Europeans), Bergson declares that he sees nothing indicating that the "primitive" does not equally understand the constant chain by which consequences follow antecedents. "Can we not say of him also," Bergson writes, "that his 'daily activity implies perfect confidence in the invariability of natural laws?'"[11] Speaking in the name of simple common sense, which above all does not wish to invent alterity where it does not exist, he continues: "Without this confidence, he would not rely on the current of the river to carry his canoe, nor on the bending of his bow to shoot his arrow, on his hatchet to cut into the trunk, on his teeth to bite, on his legs to walk."[12] And when he takes up the example Lévy-Bruhl uses to demonstrate that the "primitive" always makes recourse to "mystic causes" rather than taking account of secondary causes such as illness or the sequence of events that leads to a fatal accident, it is in order to ask the question that—beyond superficial ethnological description—is really the object: "Why?" Why erect a mystical reason as primary cause? This question thus leads him to "look more closely" to see that "what the primitive man explains here by a 'supernatural' cause is not the physical effect, it is its *human significance*," for "there is nothing illogical, consequently nothing 'prelogical'" in saying that once proximate causes have been established, "there remains to be explained this fact, so momentous to us, the death of a man."[13] It is then a fact: Listening to common sense leads back to the notion of *one* human nature. It is because of this shared human condition that we can always ask "Why?" and that we expect to see human beliefs and actions partake of the same principle of reason, which is ultimately founded upon this same condition regardless of geography and culture.

Thus Lévy-Bruhl's turn away from "primitivism" meant recognizing Bergsonian common sense and the prevalence of a human condition that cannot be divided according to irreconcilable differences in the types of reasoning. And when Lévy-Bruhl declares that if it is necessary to "continue rational efforts to understand and manage the world," it is also necessary "to recognize that without the foundation of primitive mentality (participation) we would perhaps have neither invention, nor poetry, nor even science,"[14] the primitive mentality in question is no longer *the logic of others* and thus *the other of logic*. It is humanity's shared foundation, *one* humanity's, which also shares in these "rational efforts to understand and manage the world." Emmanuel Lévinas accurately characterizes this idea, rethinking primitive mentality with the regulatory idea of *one* humanity: "The difference . . . is between two depths of the soul rather than two souls."[15]

We now come to the essential question of art. This is essential because Senghor's Negritude is first and foremost a philosophy of African art. One of Senghor's principal occupations when he arrived in Paris as a student at the end of the 1920s was visiting the Trocadéro museum. At that time, the fad for "negro art" had produced notable effects on modern art. In his *Demoiselles d'Avignon* (1907), for example, Pablo Picasso had discovered the emotion provoked in him by what he had called the "spell" of the African masks he had seen at the museum he too had visited. Moreover, just after Senghor's arrival the grand Colonial Exposition of 1931 took place, representing a moment of apotheosis for France's colonial project: The country could present itself with the spectacle of its imperial grandeur just before tipping into war and the inevitable coming decolonizations. One of the most important aspects of this exposition was that it made manifest what Benoît de l'Estoile calls a new "sensibility," by which—especially for young people, as Marcel Mauss would note—what before had been simple "fetishes" were now art objects.[16]

Indeed, it is in the domain of art that the reality of the reason-embrace that does not separate can be perceived. This is what can create—but also what can experience—the geometrical forms characteristic of African sculptures and masks, in spite of their local and regional differences. The language of reason-embrace, of the "humid and vibratory" *logos*, is spoken by these forms, which neither reproduce nor embellish reality for a gaze that would caress them from a distance. On the contrary, they contain the "obscure yet explosive" forces, in Senghor's words, that are "hidden beneath the surface of things." It is hardly surprising that Senghor would express this duality between the art produced by the principle of reason-embrace and the art produced by the reason-eye (the latter represented at its peak by Greco-Roman sculpture and its heritage) in terms of an opposition between the Dionysian and the Apollonian, nor that he sometimes makes Nietzsche part of the "1889 revolution." "He [Nietzsche] too," writes Senghor, "preaches the 'eternal return' to the symbiosis of the Apollonian spirit and the Dionysian soul, but with the emphasis on the latter. The revolution of 1889 was ripe. Let us not forget that *Thus Spoke Zarathustra* appeared in 1883–1885."[17]

Let us conclude now by returning to that offending alexandrine, not to defend Senghor but to ask what this phrase effectively meant in the context in which it was uttered. It is crucial to recognize that the text in which it appeared, "What the Black Man Contributes" (1939), not only came out of the ethnological discourse that strongly influenced Senghor in those days but was also influenced by a book that appeared ten years earlier, Paul Guillaume and Thomas Munro's *Primitive Negro Sculpture* [*La Sculpture nègre primitive*]. The fundamental idea of this book is a contrast between Greek sculpture, which solicits the caress, and African sculpture, which aims for violent emotion. In this context, Senghor's verse becomes simply: Negro sculpture is to emotion (as defined above) what Greek statuary is to the reason-eye. Whence, returning again to Lévinas, we can end by saying that the difference established between "Hellenic" and "Negro" is not a matter of two souls but two depths of the soul.

2

SENGHOR'S AFRICAN SOCIALISM

Léopold Sédar Senghor's political philosophy is continuous with his vitalist thought, stemming from the encounter that he orchestrated between the author of *Creative Evolution* and the vision of the world Senghor found in endogenous African religions. It represents what the Senegalese politician called "African socialism" or the "African road to socialism." To understand this political doctrine, it is important first to recall Senghor's political engagement, which began as early as his first years as a student in France, at the end of the 1920s. Next, we will examine his idea of an "African" reading of Karl Marx, which involves the spiritual socialism that became his philosophy when—at the same time as Marxist texts—he discovered the work of Pierre Teilhard de Chardin. And finally, we will see how this philosophy was articulated by Senghor, who became a politician at the dawn of African independence, as the task of constructing sovereign countries made it necessary to think the new notions of federalism, nationhood, the State, planning, etc.

SENGHOR'S SOCIALIST COMMITMENT

We are not used to thinking of Senghor as a figure of rebellion. Rather, it is more common to see him as a conciliatory figure, unleashing a purely poetic violence against French racist representations of Black faces smiling and declaring "y a bon banania" only so as then to produce a prayer of peace for the country, asking for it to be placed on the right hand of God the Father: This is the critique often raised against him.[1] We remember that his enthusiasm for independence was hardly overwhelming: He voted "yes" for de Gaulle in 1958 (unlike Guinean Sékou Touré), convincing the deeply nationalist Mamadou Dia to follow him and supporting the idea of a confederation between France and its African empire.[2] In other words, we tend to think of this "Black, French, and African" figure—to use the title of his American biographer, Janet Vaillant[3]—as the very illustration of an accommodation to colonialism that laid the groundwork for the neocolonialism that followed independence. This portrait is all the more accepted in that we often contrast Senghor with the other two fathers of Negritude, the Martinican Aimé Césaire and the Guyanese Léon-Gontran Damas—especially with Césaire, the constant rebel, who on the subject of accommodation declared: "Accommodate yourself to me. I won't accommodate myself to you!" In Senghor's more conciliatory attitude, Wole Soyinka sees what remains of the priest he wanted to become in his youth.[4] Occasionally Césaire would affectionately explain the difference in temperament between himself and his longtime friend by the fact that the latter was what the students at the École normale supérieure used to call a mass-goer.[5]

However, one moment in Senghor's intellectual and political life opens onto a different portrait, calling into question or at least complicating this image. This is the moment of his 1937 speech at the Dakar chamber of commerce, which would frustrate the expectations of the colonial administration that organized it. The administration hoped that Senghor, who had just returned to the country for the first time in many years, and above all was crowned in glory after having received his agrégation[6] in grammar, would present, in a public manifestation, the image of successful colonial assimilation into French culture. He was thus asked to give a speech, the content of which mattered little—or at least less, in the spirit of the organizers, than the actual person of the orator. But Senghor, speaking the language of the Harlem Renaissance, calmly delivered a compelling thesis, announcing the "new Negro" who would bring about what he called "bilingualism," broadly defined as the capacity to appropriate the French language and culture while still inhabiting the languages and cultures of Africa. We know the exhortation Senghor used to sum up this attitude: "to assimilate, not be assimilated."

Senghor would often poke fun at his own stubborn "Serer peasant" character, and this determination is the same spirit with which he had already resisted Père Lalouse, headmaster during his secondary school years at the College Libermann, who naturally considered that to civilize and to evangelize were one and the same gesture, making a blank slate of souls to be filled back in. To which the young student, speaking for his classmates, responded that it was necessary to take seriously and literally the word of the founder of his spiritual order: "Make yourselves Negroes with the Negroes to win them to Jesus Christ." Senghor wanted this phrase to be heard as what would later be the doctrine of necessary enculturation.

The picture that emerges from moments such as these is of a man setting out a certain course, from which he never deviated in the negotiations and accommodations that would follow. The most important element of this course is its commitment to an African socialism—which is also to say, a "bilingual" socialism. As his biographer Jacqueline Sorel relates, it was Senghor's schoolmate at the Lycée Louis-le-Grand, Georges Pompidou, who introduced him into socialist circles.[7] In particular, she writes, Pompidou gave him Léon Blum's articles in *Le Populaire* to read. Senghor thus became a member of the Ligue d'action universitaire républicaine et socialiste (LAURS, University Republican and Socialist Action League).[8] There he met Pierre Mendès France, as well as Edgar Faure, who would later make him secretary of state to the president of the council, in 1955, and who would receive him into the Académie française in 1984 with the apostrophe: "I will pronounce your name, Senghor!" Unlike his friend Pompidou, after these first engagements Senghor would call himself a socialist for the rest of his life. But what did "socialist" mean for this colonized—mass-going—Catholic?

A SPIRITUALIST AND VITALIST SOCIALISM

If Senghor's initial socialist engagement took place before the war, it was after World War Two that the thought that would be developed at the beginning of the 1960s as his doctrine of African socialism took root in the poet. The moment immediately after the war was the moment at which he "fell into politics," as he put it, becoming a Senegalese representative in the French parliament. Along with many others, at that time he discovered the writings of the "young Marx," collected under the title of the *1844 Manuscripts* in reference to the year when they had been completed in Paris; they were then abandoned to the "gnawing criticism of the mice" before their eventual publication in Leipzig in 1932. Finally, this was the moment when he discovered and read the work of Pierre Teilhard de Chardin. When we put these different moments together, we see the outlines of Senghor's thought begin to emerge: Senghor read Marx with the eyes of Teilhard de Chardin, who in many respects echoed the Bergsonian philosophy shown to be at the heart of Senghor's thought in the previous chapter.

We know Louis Althusser's thesis concerning Marx's early work, which—according to him—represents the prehistory of the more properly scientific work of constituting what he called the "Continent of History." Between the *1844 Manuscripts* and the mature works that followed *Capital*, there is an epistemological break that meant, among other things, that what was sought on one side of it in uncertain language and terminology would later be formulated on the other side of the break, and thanks to it, in scientific discourse. Thus, what was first tentatively thought under the notion of *alienation* could now come to its full theoretical and practical effectiveness as the concept of *surplus value*. Philosophy could be replaced by science, and the interpretation of the world could give way to its transformation.

It is precisely because he shares the same premise—that an abyss separates the Marx of the *Manuscripts* from the mature Marx—that Senghor absolutely opposes Althusser's thinking here. According to Senghor, the philosopher of 1844 is the real Marx, who would later betray himself in a certain scientific positivism that was in the air of his time. The Marx adopted by Senghor, and on whom he would base his spiritualist socialism, is the philosopher of alienation and not the economist of surplus value.[9] And when Senghor thinks of "alienation," for him this is a matter both of the human condition in general and of colonized humanity in particular. In "Marxism and Humanism," which appeared several months after the French publication of the *Manuscripts*, Senghor writes:

> For us, men of 1947, men living after two world wars, we who have just escaped the bloodthirsty contempt of dictators and who are threatened by other dictators, what profit is to be had from these works of youth! Indeed they encapsulate the ethical principles of Marx, who proposes as the object of our practical activity the total liberation of man.[10]

As a Bergsonian and a Teilhardian, how does Senghor interpret Marx's concept of alienation? Let us cite one of Marx's own definitions in the chapter of the *Manuscripts* entitled "Alienated Work":

> The worker is related to the *product of his labor* as to an *alien* object. . . . The more the worker expends himself in work the more powerful becomes the world of objects which he creates in face of himself, the poorer he becomes in his inner life, and the less he belongs to himself. It is just the same as in religion. The more of himself man attributes to God the less he has left in himself. The worker puts his life into the object and his life then belongs no longer to himself but to the object. . . . . The *alienation* of the worker in his product means not only that his labor

> becomes an object, assumes an *external* existence, but that it exists independently, *outside himself*, and alien to him, and that it stands opposed to him as an autonomous power. The life which he has given to the object sets itself against him as an alien and hostile force.[11]

Senghor frequently indicated the necessity of an African rereading of Marx even as he was sometimes derided from the left for what could seem like a lack of substance vis-à-vis a "scientific" socialism. Let us, though, move through Senghor's reading of the well-known passage cited above. To define alienation, as Marx does here, as the loss of some vital substance to the profit of an external, alien, and hostile object in effect corresponds to Senghor's vitalist philosophy. As previously stated, this philosophy represents the encounter between the ontology of forces that underlies African religions of different regions—their common denominator, so to speak—and the Bergsonian notion of "vital force" [*élan vital*]. Thus, the following principles apply:

1. To be is to be a force of life.
2. What reinforces the being-force is good.
3. What de-forces it (*dé-forcer* is Senghor's neologism in French), what—like a vampire—sucks out the vital substance that it is, is bad.
4. All force naturally strives to be *more force*—or in different terms, the goal of being is to become *more being.*

This fourth principle—this conatus of the vital substance—echoes the emergent cosmology or cosmogenesis theorized by Teilhard de Chardin, as is signaled by the expression "more being." If Senghor consistently returns to the theologian/philosopher's works, starting from the moment of his discovery of them onward, this is because Teilhard represents for him the completion of what he found in Bergson as the philosophy of vital push and in Marx as the philosophy of a total liberation of the human from his state of alienation in order to bring about a true humanism. In a text called "Homage to Teilhard de Chardin," he wrote that Marx was largely unaware of "us"; by "us," he meant the colonized African people. By contrast, he declared, the author of *The Phenomenon of Man* was himself far enough removed from Eurocentrism to think what he called a "socialization of the earth," which would "totalize the Earth," bringing about as the *humanization* of the planet the process that began with its "*hominization*." In this cosmology of emergence, the push toward more being is carried out. Its horizon is what Senghor, always a Teilhardian, consistently refers to as "Civilization of the universal."

We will conclude with Senghor's Teilhardian Marxism by insisting on four points. The first returns to Marx's definition of alienation as the loss of vital substance to the profit of an exterior object in which the worker no longer recognizes himself. After having spoken of it as "loss of reality" and "loss of the object," and also of "dispossession," in these lines Marx presents alienation as more like vampirization: a case, in other words, of what Senghor calls "de-forcement."

The second point is the fact that, for Senghor, socialism is in the cosmogenetic order of the movement of the world, so to speak. More than a choice of ideology or an economic system in which the course of things is not left to the free play of market forces, socialism means something like the ethical choice to proceed in the direction of the push of life toward "more being," always toward more humanism. This explains the title Senghor gave to his 1948 article, "Marxism and Humanism." Instead of Senghor himself, let us quote here his partner and intellectual accomplice (before their disastrous separation), Mamadou Dia, the other "father" of the Senegalese nation:

> *If it is required to act, it is in order to become, to be more being.* For industrial creation to be a good, and not the ruin of man, it must keep a human element; it must not bring about a new slavery under the pretext of productivity or efficiency; it must not give rise to a progress that is only perversion or a thirst for *well being* but *not* for *more* being; it must not produce a world in which ethics is effaced before power, spirit before matter, a world of inanimate objects.[12]

The third point concerns the spiritualist aspect of Senghor's socialism. For him, an affinity with the young Marx rather than the Marx of *Capital* permits a version of socialism that needs neither atheism nor materialism. Concerning atheism, obviously Senghor attends closely to the passage in "Alienated Work" in which Marx portrays religion not as an ideological apparatus (the "opium of the people") but as a factor of "de-forcement": the human transfers the vital substance of which she thus deprives herself to the divine. (This is the theme Feuerbach develops in *The Essence of Christianity.*) It is then upheld that humanism must necessarily construct itself against the theological in a zero-sum game in which one side only wins what the other loses. In response to this, Senghor contends that Marx's objection to religious alienation can actually be considered as a "reaction originating in Christianity against historical Christian deviations" that "left untouched the very essence of the religion all the more so that the idea of alienation itself originates in religion." Consequently, Senghor declares, religion and the movement of liberation from alienation fight the same fight; and he specifies that this is true for both Christian and Muslim religions.[13] It is therefore unnecessary to see an opposition between the theological and humanism. Indeed, the contrary is true, provided that religion reclaims its own nature as a movement of liberation of the human, who can then cultivate the creative force that is his very being. As opposed to a humanism that comes about only with the death of God, Senghor wants to think a humanism nourished by the Living and defined as collaboration with God to bring about the completion of creation, not against Him. It is because of this conception of humanism that Senghor's philosophy finds a kindred thinking in the philosophy of Muhammad Iqbal, whom he would call a "Muslim Teilhard." The idea that the human collaborates with God in the activity of the continuous creation of an open world is in effect at the heart of Iqbal's thought (which Senghor likely discovered around 1955, the year when the Indian poet's major work, *The Reconstruction of Religious Thought in Islam*, was published in the French translation by Eva de Vitray-Meyerovitch). Finally, for Senghor materialism is also not consubstantial with socialism: From Teilhard he learned to overcome the dualism of matter and spirit, to which he substituted instead the monism of energy.

The fourth and last important point concerns art—as one would expect, because it is impossible to overemphasize the point to which all aspects of Senghor's thought, theory of intuitive knowledge, ontology of vital force, and politics are all developments of his philosophy of African art.

So Senghor is a socialist. Unlike his friend Aimé Césaire, a militant of the French Communist Party up until the publication of his thunderous letter of resignation to Maurice Thorez in 1956,[14] Senghor would never be drawn to communism, devout as he was. But it was not only a matter of religion; there was also the foil of the aesthetic philosophy of socialist realism and what it seemed to him to indicate about the nature of Soviet communism as a factor of de-forcement.[15]

For Senghor, the cosmic movement of shaking free from all alienation—which is to say, going toward *more-*

being—is what brings about the creative human or, in other words, the artist. It is in art that we can find a premonition of what it is we must become. The repossession of the self signifies the capacity to "produce only in freedom" and to "create in accordance with the laws of beauty," in the phrases from Marx that recur often in Senghor's work. According to his Teilhardian Marxism, the poet sees evolution as movement toward liberation (cosmic and political), from *homo faber* to *homo artifex*, via *homo sapiens* along the way.

However, socialist realism eventually ends up meaning absence of liberty. When Senghor responds to those who criticize him in the name of real or scientific socialism, he does so by invoking what he sees as the philosophy expressed in African art, which, he explains, is an aesthetic of *subrealism*: The work of art aims not to show beautiful Apollonian appearance but to capture the Dionysian force that is the object in itself beneath the reality it presents to the gaze. According to Senghor, the young African intellectuals and artists who critique him from the left betray themselves in Soviet communism, just as they betray themselves, on the aesthetic level, in an art that makes realism into a norm.

FEDERAL STATE, NATION, PLANNING

As a statesman charged with the highest responsibilities during the wave of independences at the end of the 1950s, Senghor was led not only to think what he called the "African road to socialism" politically and philosophically but to try to construct it. For him, the work of construction would first need a federation, without which separate independences would never be more than nominal. Thus, he wrote in his 1959 report to the constitutive congress of the Parti de la fédération of Mali:[16]

> As a matter of fact, we are *independent* in the etymological sense of the word. As we have said, independence is essentially nondependence in one's decisions: *freedom to choose.* We were free to choose on September 28, 1958. We are still, at any moment, free to choose the road to our destiny. . . . Let us continue our analysis of the concept of independence. Our first observation is that, like any concept, it does not embrace all reality, but simplifies it dangerously to the extent that it becomes a legal term. For a jurist, independence is a *form*, not a reality. The independent state is one that is so recognized, *de jure*, internationally. To a lesser degree, it is that state that has the external signs of sovereignty: an army and diplomacy, I do not even say a currency. Now there are armies and armies, diplomacies and diplomacies. Those of the Big Two are really armies and diplomacies. Who would dare affirm that those of a given "dwarf-state" in Asia or Africa really are? In other words, legal independence is indeed nominal and not necessarily *real*.[17]

As we can see, if Senghor is not necessarily hastening toward independence, this is because there were things more urgent than legal sovereignty—complete with army, flag, and diplomacy—at this particular moment: It was necessary to reconstitute the vast ensembles that might be able to heal the curse of "dwarf-states." This curse was the continuation of alienation. On this point, let us return again to Senghor's speech:

> A purely nominal independence is a false one. It may satisfy national pride, but it does not eliminate the awareness of alienation, the frustration, and the inferiority complex, since it cannot resolve the concrete problems confronting the under-developed countries: housing, clothing, feeding, curing, and educating the masses. . . . As we have seen, Federation, generally speaking, is our major means.[18]

It is useful to keep the topicality of Senghor's address in mind at our contemporary moment, when a majority of African nations have celebrated the fiftieth anniversary of their independence—remembering that the celebration, necessary as it certainly is, should not at all obfuscate the fact that the promises of development that accompanied independence are hardly realized today. Senghor was right to contend, not without bitterness after the failures of various attempts to keep the African states together in some greater whole, that "the United States of Africa" for which he said that he struggled was not "for tomorrow":

> We were naïve to believe that a federation was possible in 1959 between states that had been *disunited* in 1957. We underestimated the present strength of territorialism, of micro-nationalism, in Africa. We forgot to analyze and understand the sociological differences among the territories of what used to be French West Africa, differences that the colonial administration had reinforced. This takes priority over personal ambitions and the nations' race to *leadership*.[19]

Without getting bogged down in imprecations—for he knew perfectly well the force of sociological circumstances but also the degree to which Africans themselves were at fault in the Balkanization of their states—Senghor underscored that France had added to the wrongdoings of colonization by having first "dis-united" before decolonization, which made the future darker.[20] And even today, Senghor is still justified in having set the task for following generations as "regroup[ing] the independent African states on the basis of regional and cultural affinities"—for, once again, "one cannot develop a nation in the narrow framework of its territorial limits. The facts are there that prove it, as are the European, American, and Asian efforts."[21]

To make populations into one people, to be the "father of a nation" in the concrete situation of the time of independence: This meant founding a community that recognizes its reality, starting from the embryonic state represented by colonial administration. Here the state is neither the emanation of the nation nor the expression of the class struggle but the principle that establishes the people. In the context of decolonization, it is not nationalism that wills and creates the state. On the contrary, the state establishes the people. The "fathers of nations" in Africa were constrained, forced, to adopt a Hegelian philosophy of the state. Here we can think of the way Hegel opposes Fries in the preface to his *Elements of the Philosophy of Right*. For Hegel, the truth "with regards to ethical ideals, the state, the government, and the constitution" does not "ascend out of each man's heart, feeling, and enthusiasm" and the state is not born out of "the brew and stew of the 'heart, friendship, and enthusiasm.'"[22]

Thus we can understand why Senghor never considered Balkanization, or the separate independences of the former French possessions in West Africa following the "natural" inclinations of these territories and their people, as a fatal flaw. His political conceptions about the constitution of peoples and nations starting from the state explains that he might have considered that starting from the French colonial administration to build Senegal, or the Federation of Mali, or the Union of West African States, were all aspects of the same project. Certainly, this entailed a disregard for the classes and their struggle, as the notion of a people served to erase their reality. This is explained by the idea, shared with fellow theorists such as Kwame Nkrumah and Julius Nyerere, that African Socialism founded on community rather than class was already anticipated in the "communion of souls rather than the aggregation of individuals," which was for him traditional African society. Did he ignore the ethnic differences whose damages are still visible in Africa today and the challenges they posed to the democratization of the States of the continent? Ethnicity did nothing to weaken his belief in the inaugural power of the state. It is true that attachment to the "fatherland"—by which Senghor meant something like "region" (so there is a Serer fatherland, a Malinke fatherland, a Baoulé, a Fon)—is a "natural determination" for populations. But for him, it is equally true that the élan vital toward more-being brings these fatherlands together in order to transcend them. Citing Hegel, Senghor writes: "Once achieved, the nation forges a harmonious ensemble out of its different provinces: a single country for a single people, animated by one faith and striving towards the same goal. In the words of Hegel . . . 'It is not the natural determinations of the nation that form its character, but rather its national spirit.'"[23]

Decades later, today the project of African union has again come to the fore. This why we must reread Senghor on the establishment of the people out of the matrix of meaning that is the state. Senghor showed that the notion of an African people is not a fixed identity but a *program*. It is a manner of thinking the idea of a "constitutional patriotism," to cite Jürgen Habermas.

We should not end a discussion of Senghor's political philosophy without mention of the importance of prospective thought, in which Senghor doubtless also heard the echo of a Bergsonian philosophy of time. Of course his African socialism emphasized the virtues of planning. But a plan, for the disciple of Gaston Berger Senghor considered himself, was first a prospective project. What does it mean to inscribe planning within prospective?

First, this is not the type of planning which constrains the future by setting out numbers to be achieved through voluntarism. It is about finding, with Gaston Berger—himself in agreement with Bergson on this point—the sense of "open time": "The philosopher who has contributed the most to shaking the static representations of the world and to 'opening up' our conception of time is probably Henri Bergson. The originality of his work does not lie so much in certain distinctions he introduced and which have become classic . . . but in the fact that in his work the traditional concept of time was exploded for the first time. The future is no longer what must unavoidably take place; it is not even what will happen; it is what the whole world will do."[24]

Retrieving the sense of open time in this way means understanding prospective as the attitude of the spirit that is oriented toward the future, which leads to action according to the principle that its meaning comes from the future. In other words, it is the vision of the possible future, the "futurable," to use the language of prospective, that dictates what must be done in the present.

An insistence on this prospective attitude also means, for Senghor, the rejection of attempts to lean on ethnology in order to affirm that African cultures are characterized by a closed vision of time, one without much future. The idea that "the future is not just the present extended" and that "we must look at the future not as starting with the present but from the vantage point of the future itself,"[25] as Berger wrote: This is the foundation of Senghor's philosophy of time and the vision of planning he shares with Mamadou Dia.[26] This Bergsonian philosophy of time is also at the core of Muhammad Iqbal's work.

3

BERGSON, IQBAL, AND THE CONCEPT OF *IJTIHAD*

In a 1931 letter to Sir William Rosenstein, Muhammad Iqbal narrates a trip to Paris, along with another Indian friend, to see Bergson. Iqbal recounts that although Bergson was ill and not receiving visitors, he made an exception and spent two full hours with his guests. Iqbal writes that their conversation included discussion of Berkeley's philosophy, among other subjects. Louis Massignon, whom Iqbal also visited in 1932 during the same trip, relates the Indian poet's Parisian encounters:

> Iqbal knew Bergson previously, and despite a terrible English translation (repudiated by Bergson) had come to feel a "Semitic" spiritual affinity for Bergson, so ended up coming to Paris to converse with him. But he also wanted to talk to me about Hallaj. He wrote me on 2/18/1932 from Lahore: "I am sending you a copy of (my) latest work 'Javid Nama' which I hope

> will interest you, especially the part relating Hallaj and Nietzsche. . . . I have allowed the former to explain himself, and as to the latter I have tried to show how a Muslim Mystic would look at him. The book is a kind of Divine Comedy of Islam. It is a pity I was not able to meet you in London. I am now thinking of making a tour to Spanish Morocco and if possible to French Morocco. This will give me an opportunity to meet you in Paris." In fact I saw him at my home on November 1st, 1932.[1]

It is difficult to say exactly what Massignon intends by "'Semitic' spiritual affinity"—but it ran very deep, whatever it was. To understand this, and to understand to what point Iqbal thought *as a Bergsonian*, we must first remember that Bergson was widely translated after the publication of *Creative Evolution* in 1907 and its immense success. In particular, his work appeared in England after 1911. Muhammad Iqbal had himself defended his philosophy thesis, *The Development of Metaphysics in Persia*, at Cambridge in 1907. He set himself the task of producing his philosophy of the "reconstruction" of Islamic thought, first in poetry, starting in 1915; this was the publication date of his long metaphysical poem written in Persian, *The Secrets of the Self.* At that time, he was already familiar with Bergsonian categories.

It seems likely that, by speaking of a "Semitic" affinity, Massignon wanted to symbolize what this meeting between Bergson and the Muslim Indian represented.

Especially at the present moment, it is well worth coming back to that symbol in order to emphasize the value of the dialogue in which the philosopher—attracted to Catholicism, almost to the point of conversion, but at the same time remaining true to his Jewish faith—inspired the Muslim Indian in his project of rethinking Quranic cosmology in order to give a new meaning to the juridico-theological concept of *ijtihad*, usually translated as "effort of interpretation"—a concept that we can agree is necessary for our contemporary era.

We will focus first on the figure of Muhammad Iqbal: in particular, on his status as a "founding father" of Pakistan and the role he played in the partition of India at the moment of independence. We will turn next to Iqbal's thought, connecting it back to a number of theses we will explain. Finally, we will explore Iqbal's philosophy of action and *ijtihad*.

MUHAMMAD IQBAL AND THE BIRTH OF PAKISTAN

Muhammad Iqbal was born on November 9, 1877, in the Punjabi city of Sialkot. His family, of Brahmin origin, came from Kashmir. Indeed, in his book *The Discovery of India*, Pandit Jawaharlal Nehru emphasizes Iqbal's identity as a Kashmiri Brahmin, most likely to indicate the presence of a common Hindu culture despite the separatism that would divide independent India, and in which Iqbal would play a crucial role. After his education at Murray College in Sialkot and a brief stint as a teacher at Lahore College, where he formed a friendship with the orientalist and philosopher Sir Thomas Arnold (1864–1930), he went to England to continue his studies at Cambridge in 1905. There he pursued philosophy and law, receiving a law degree and defending his dissertation (*The Development of Metaphysics in Persia: A Contribution to the History of Muslim Philosophy*) in 1907. This thesis would be published the next year with a dedication to Professor Arnold, thanking him for a decade of training in the essentials of philosophy.

It is important to note that Iqbal's intellectual trajectory diverges significantly from that of another modernist thinker, Jamāl al-Dīn al-Afghānī (1838–1897), who died three years before the beginning of the twentieth century. The latter emphasized the importance of philosophy as the true condition of modernity; technology was only a consequence, albeit a particularly visible one. Consequently, he lamented that the teaching of philosophy where it still existed—that is, in the Shia world he inhabited—had remained largely Neoplatonist, stuck in the paradigm of Aristotelian cosmology, or that of a finite world. Al-Afghānī was an activist above all, and although he produced several philosophical texts, he did not have Muhammad Iqbal's training in modern Western philosophy. Thus although he called on the intellectual elite of the Islamic world to move from a closed world to an infinite universe—to cite Alexandre Koyré's well-known title—he did not have the means to lay out the consequences of this for a "reconstruction of the religious thought of Islam" as fully as Iqbal did—much less the time, considering the tumultuous life he led. We can cite the following passage, from an article on the utility of philosophy. Here he rebukes the Indian intelligentsia who in his estimation have betrayed their mission by not having understood that true fidelity is movement, not some foundational identity that one must stubbornly guard against time:

> Is it not incumbent upon you to serve those who will follow you with your highest thoughts, just as your revered predecessors served you? . . . Is it not a fault for a percipient sage not to learn the entire sphere of new sciences and inventions and fresh creations, when he has no information about their causes and reasons? And when the world has changed from a state to another and he does not raise his hand from the sleep of neglect?[2]

Two points stand out about this passage. The first is that al-Afghānī's attitude here explains his profound agreement with the ideas put forward by Ernest Renan in his famous conference on Islam and science, which took place at the Sorbonne in 1883 on the occasion of the visit to Paris by the man he called "Afghan sheik," an account of which was later published in *Le Journal des débats*. Al-Afghānī did not wish to produce a song of the brilliance of Islamic civilization in its golden age in order to oppose Renan's views of apparent lack of scientific spirit in the Islamic world. Instead, what he wanted was the

Muslim societies *of his time* to cease to prove correct the author of *The Future of Science.*

The second point is that al-Afghānī's aim in speaking of the "effects" of the new sciences doubtless includes technology but concerns, above all, the profound transformation of mental categories, such as our conceptions of time and space. This is also what Iqbal says in his assessment of the point to which modern sciences require a new conception of time. This is the importance of Bergsonian philosophy of vital push and duration for him, as he sets about understanding Quranic cosmology as continuous emergence and thus the necessity of perpetual renewal to accord with the very movement of life. In opposition to the jurists' obsession with condemning all "innovation" as naturally blameworthy, for Iqbal it is necessary to take into account that life itself is innovation. To live is to change continually.

Before returning to this point, the Bergsonian heart of Iqbal's thought, we will turn back to the events that made Iqbal into the father of Pakistan, or one of them. After completing his studies, he returned to India to work as a lawyer, which naturally led him—given the colonial era in which he lived—to enter into politics. At a moment in which Hindu and Muslim nationalisms mirrored each other as they developed, it was also natural that his intervention would take place in the project of the All India Muslim League, especially after the blow to the Khilafat movement constituted by the abolition of the institution of the caliphate by Kemal Atatürk's Turkey in 1924. In 1926, Iqbal was elected a member of the Punjab Legislative Assembly. It was as president of the Muslim League that, at the League's twenty-fifth annual session on December 29, 1930, he gave a speech that has remained historic, perceived as the act that brought about the birth of the separate state of Pakistan. In fact, in this speech, Iqbal speaks of the necessary autonomy of majority Muslim regions in an Indian Federation. He does not mention independence, and it was probably not independence that he had in mind. Nevertheless, this speech marks the moment at which the idea of Pakistan took shape. Besides, had not Iqbal once declared: "Nations are born in the hearts of poets; they prosper and die in the hands of politicians"?[3]

The main points Iqbal elaborated in his presidential address are as follows. First, he affirms that Islam as a culture—which is to say, a legal system centered on a specific ideal of life—establishes a political community. Second, he notes the development of a European modernity that, in its spread, has tended to universalize the model of the nation-state as the particular ethical ideal in which the territory becomes the principle of solidarity. The consequence of this development, which is partly the result of the Reformation, has been the privatization of religion. In contrast to this state of things—this is the third point of Iqbal's remarks—it is important to note that Islam does not separate what is into a duality of spirit and matter: "In Islam," he declares,

> God and the universe, spirit and matter, Church and State, are organic to each other. Man is not the citizen of a profane world to be renounced in the interest of a world of spirit situated elsewhere. To Islam, matter is spirit realizing itself in space and time.[4]

According to Iqbal, the European nationalist conception—nationalist in the sense of its inscription of cultural, social, and political life at the heart of and within the boundaries of the nation—is to be contrasted with the vision of Islam about which he declares: "*Islam is itself destiny and will not suffer a destiny.*"[5] This somewhat enigmatic proclamation can be interpreted to mean that Islam is in itself a principle of organization and movement, which cannot let itself be organized from the outside by the principle of the nation-state. Addressing the members of the Muslim League, he adds that this is the reason that "your future as a distinct cultural unit in India" is an important issue at stake—for the question, he explains, is this:

> Is it possible to retain Islam as an ethical ideal and to reject it as a polity, in favor of national polities in which [the] religious attitude is not permitted to play any part? This question becomes of special importance in India, where the Muslims happen to be a minority. The proposition that religion is a private individual experience is not surprising on the lips of a European.[6]

Citing Renan's definition of the nation as moral conscience, he describes the caste, ethnic, and religious communities of India before continuing: "The unity of an Indian nation, therefore, must be sought not in the negation, but in the mutual harmony and cooperation, of the many."[7] Next, he sets out the principle according to which "each group is entitled to its free development on its own lines."[8] Even the authors of the "Nehru report" must have recognized this, he continues—in other words, even those who shared the philosophy of the pandit, believing in a homogenous India in which secularism would confine religion to the private sphere and only the identity of citizenship would be tolerated in the public sphere.

Reading the presentation of this principle today, we cannot help but note that the evils of South African apartheid were defined in much the same terms: Development can only occur in separation. For Iqbal, the consequence that follows from the principle is that the Muslim demand for the creation of a Muslim India at the heart of India is perfectly justified. "Personally," he declares in the lines that would become the historical heart of his speech,

> I would go farther. . . . *I would like to see the Punjab, North-West Frontier Province, Sind and Baluchistan amalgamated into a single State. Self-government within the British Empire, or without the British Empire, the formation of a consolidated North-West Indian*

Muslim State appears to me to be the final destiny of the Muslims, at least of North-West India.[9]

Once again, what Iqbal speaks of is only an autonomous development at the heart of the political whole that is India—but we know what would come about seventeen years later. What to make of this? Should we see Iqbal as the one who sowed the grain of separatism and who even convinced Muhammad Ali Jinnah to follow this path? Or is he the poet-philosopher who proclaimed his opposition to the "idols of the race and the tribe?" Nehru, who came to visit him on his deathbed, recounts in *The Discovery of India* having said to him at the end of their conversation: "Jinnah is a politician, but you are a poet."

At the beginning of his speech, Iqbal presents himself as a man without much political experience who leads no party and follows no leader. He speaks only, he says, as a student of "the spirit of Islam, as it unfolds itself in time."[10] He aims for one single goal: starting from his sense of this movement, to shed light on the principle on which the league should base its decisions. The response to questions about the direction of Iqbal's approach can be found in the way he introduces it here. In a word, it is his reflection on the necessity of *ijtihad* in Islam—on the necessary reactivation of the principle of movement that is, for him, Muslim culture itself—that leads him to the idea that the Muslim community of India had a crucial role to play, given its demography in particular. It could only play this role if it enjoyed autonomy of decision-making and orientation to create the conditions for this critical self-reappraisal, slipping into the movement of life. Autonomy was the sine qua non for this, since it would be difficult to imagine a Muslim "caucus" within a unified Indian parliament, which would have neither legitimacy nor force to act upon the course of things. And Iqbal insisted upon the fact that a Muslim state (or, rather, a state of Muslims) did not mean an Islamic state, evoking an article from the *Times of India* on this point in the following terms:

> The character of a Muslim State can be judged from what the *Times of India* pointed out some time ago in a leader on the Indian Banking Inquiry Committee. "In ancient India," the paper points out, "the State framed laws regulating the rates of interest; but in Muslim times, although Islam clearly forbids the realization of interest on money loaned, Indian Muslim States imposed no restrictions on such rates." I therefore demand the formation of a consolidated Muslim State in the best interests of India and Islam.[11]

Even if he says nothing very specific about his vision for this "Muslim" autonomous state, it is clear that the spirit of Iqbal's speech is to make space for *ijtihad*, understood as the invention of practices and rules that are adapted to circumstances, and also to modernity, not the imposition of legislation that was intended to apply at all times in all places, a manner of seeing that Iqbal calls an "Arabian imperialism": "for Islam, an opportunity to rid itself of the stamp that Arabian Imperialism was forced to give it, to mobilize its law, its education, its culture, and to bring them into closer contact with its own original spirit and with the spirit of modern times."[12]

To "mobilize" here means to put back into movement—for it is indeed his vitalist philosophy, the site of his "spiritual affinity" with Bergson, that inspires him here. This philosophy can be summarized in the eight following theses:

1. To be is to become an individual.
2. There is an ontological scale of beings, according to the degree of consistency of their individuality.
3. Only God is an accomplished individual, an Ego.
4. As God's lieutenant, the human is the being who is entrusted with the deposit of personality, or the capacity to realize oneself as an individual.
5. This self-realization as individual or person comes about in and by action (as opposed to contemplation or reflection in meditation).
6. To create oneself in action means, for the human, to fulfill the mission to be a collaborator with God in the work of the completion of creation.
7. The field of human action is an open, living world, perpetually becoming, where newness is perpetually produced.
8. The principle of movement—in other words, the affirmation that life is innovation—is the very meaning of what in Islam is called *ijtihad*.

Theses one through four introduce Iqbal's ontology, on which his philosophy of action and *ijtihad* (five through eight) is founded.

IQBAL'S ONTOLOGY

At the foundation of Iqbal's thought is the following principle of Leibnizian *monadology*: "I hold this identical proposition, differentiated only by the emphasis, to be an axiom, namely, *that what is not truly **one** being is not truly one **being** either.*"[13] Iqbal indicates that in fact there is one grand alternative in philosophy, which leads to different consequences: Spinozistic monism or Leibnizian pluralism. Spinozistic monism leads to the mystical thesis of the reabsorption of beings into the only Being who is. Ontological pluralism, by contrast, is the affirmation that the individual exists, that to be is to be an individual. Iqbal's project rests on this affirmation. Turning his back on a Sufism of contemplation, the end of which is absorption in the one existing totality, he insists on a Sufism of the value of the human ego.

It is within the frame of this project that the Bergsonian thought of individuation takes on its full importance. At the beginning of *Creative Evolution*, Bergson considers the tendency to individualize as the very nature of organic life, explaining that it coexists with its opposite, which is the tendency toward reproduction. The process of becoming-individual, he says, harbors in itself its "enemy," its opposite, which is the tendency toward repetition.[14] Thus the only accomplished individual is God, who is the Ego or the Self, as Iqbal calls him. In his first long metaphysical poem in Persian, *The Secrets of the Self* (1915), it is precisely this self-becoming that is at issue. The poet rejects the tradition of a certain Sufism that holds that the self is something detestable, is evil in person, and at the same time the illusion that it is necessary to dissolve. He thus reverses the poetic images by which this idea has been expressed in the mystical literature of Islam: the moth whose destiny is annihilation in the flame, the drop of water yearning to disappear into the sea.

In the *Reconstruction*, Iqbal revisits the experience of the Sufi Al-Ḥallāj and his famous statement, "I am the Truth," that led him to the gallows, changing perspectives from the one he adopted in his dissertation, *Metaphysics in Persia*. In *Metaphysics in Persia*, he explains Ḥallāj's logion by saying that in him, it was infinity itself that testified to the self, as in the Mosaic experience of the burning bush (there is no other God before me = I am that I am). From a different direction, that of the ontological pluralism developed in the *Reconstruction*, the self experiences the self in its consistency *sub quadam specie aeternitatis*. The self absorbs the infinite—that is to say, the lordly attributes. Thus, a philosophy of the loss of self is replaced by a philosophy of the realization of the self.

Iqbal's philosophy of becoming-individual does not come only from Bergson. It is buttressed also on the Sufi tradition of the *Insân al-kâmil, homo perfectus*, of whom the Prophet of Islam is the example par excellence. More specifically, we can say that Iqbal's philosophy organizes the meeting of Bergsonian thought of becoming-individual and this Sufi tradition, founded among other things on the Quranic verse that, speaking of the prophetic experience that leads Muhammad into the presence of God, says: "His look never wavered" (62:17). According to Iqbal, this unwavering look manifests the meaning of the affirmation of itself by the finite individual, of the consistency of the atom even in the presence of the sun.

The human, therefore, is the being closest to God, closer even than those "brought closer" who are the angels. On the scale of beings defined by their degree of what Iqbal calls "I am-ness" (the power to say "I am"), the human occupies the summit, and this explains his creation as God's caliph—his lieutenant, or vicegerent. The deposit he receives and to which he owes his position is, according to Iqbal, that of personality.

PHILOSOPHY OF ACTION AND *IJTIHAD*

The degree of "I am-ness," of individuation, is not given. It is always becoming, in an open process, and its completion comes about through action, not through contemplation or the reflexive grasp of the self. To explain all these aspects, Iqbal coins the concept of "ego-activity": The ego is activity in a world that is itself continually emerging. How does such a vitalism correspond to the Quranic cosmology? For Iqbal, Islamic thought's encounter with Greek thought was its greatest gift but also its greatest misfortune, since Greek and Hellenistic thought led it down the path of contemplation, itself linked to a static cosmology: If God's creative act is finished and posed as such, there is nothing left to do but "find it good," as it is written in the book of Genesis, and to contemplate what has been made from nothing. However, Iqbal says, Bergson's thought in particular—the thought of the world as vital push and time as duration—today teaches us to understand the dynamic cosmology of a continuous creation, which, he says, is truly the Quran's. Among the many possible citations supporting this affirmation, Iqbal frequently quotes these two: "He adds to His creation what He wills" (35:1) and "See they not how God bringeth forth creation? and then causeth it to return again? This truly is easy for God. Say, go through the earth, and see how he hath brought forth created beings. Hereafter, with a second birth will God cause them to be born again; for God is Almighty" (29:19–20). He also often cites the Prophetic tradition (hadith), "Do not vilify time, for time is God."

So we have an open world, a world in which God's creative act is always at work, rather than withdrawing from the world and abandoning it to its mechanisms. We know that in the Newtonian system, God remains present, coming back from time to time to wind the clock again. Pierre-Simon Laplace's *Celestial Mechan-*

ics no longer needed this "hypothesis," or so the savant declared to Napoleon. In such a world, the human achieves the realization of the self by transforming it continuously, cocreating it with God. What would it mean to "vilify time"? It would mean to consider time the enemy of being—to consider that the first generation of "pious ancestors" represented perfection, from which could only follow various figures of the loss of this original meaning (a collapse continuing from "the Followers" to "the Followers of the Followers," etc.). Consequently, one must push back against time, in the retrospective stubbornness necessary for salvation; innovation can only be blameworthy, for all newness is by definition loss, the only good being fidelity conceived as static imitation.

Bergson's vitalist philosophy permits an escape from this paradigm. The model is no longer that of a celestial mechanics but living ferment where vital push is ceaselessly at work. Life being newness (God being every day engaged in a new creation), human action consists in keeping up continuously with the movement of life. Thus, what it means for Islam to deploy its modernity is not a question of technique, of engineering adaption to something external to oneself called "modernity." The concept of a "reconstruction" of Islamic thought is not to be understood as adaptation or imitation (of an external model or even of itself, in the will to self-reproduce) but as the resumption of a principle of movement, and thus an escape from the petrification that happened in the thirteenth century. This is the grand, cosmic definition of *ijtihad*, one that goes well beyond its purely juridical meaning. This is the reason we can say that the *mujtahid* (the one who produces the effort of interpretation) is nothing other than the *mujadid* (the one who renews, who brings about rebirth). We must also add that this is not a matter of individuals, or "heroes," so much as it is of sociopolitical—and therefore cultural—movements.

What is *ijtihad* on a strictly juridical level? In general, it is explained by evoking the name of Mu'adh ibn Jabal and the prophetic tradition about him. This tradition says that before sending him to Yemen to instruct local populations in the Islamic religion to which they had just converted, Muhammad wanted to be sure of his approach to the living reality he would have to teach. He asked Mu'adh, "How will you judge?" "I will judge according to the Quran," he answered. The Prophet responded, "And if you find no answer therein?" Mu'adh said, "Then I will judge by the tradition of the Prophet of God." The Prophet asked, "And if you find no answer therein?" Mu'adh said, "Then I will freely use reason in the effort of forming my own judgment."

To this tradition, we can also add the one declaring that when a jurisprudent follows independent reasoning and reaches a correct conclusion, he obtains a double reward; but if after a course of independent reasoning his conclusion is incorrect, he still receives a reward all the same. Both traditions insist on the value of reasoning that admits the new. The most important part of the

Prophet's interrogation of Mu'adh is the refusal of the "all is said" attitude, which is exactly the posture of those who push back against time. It is not a matter of bringing the unknown back to the known, flattening the new down upon what serves as legal precedent. Instead, at stake is the affirmation of a radical newness that literally has no precedent.

This is indeed Iqbal's sense of things, and it is in this emergent cosmology that he understands the response to the radically new as *ijtihad*. It is also the point of view from which he judges the draconian conditions put in place by the jurists for the exercise of this interpretive effort. Why did legal schools impose on the *mujtahid* the knowledge of all the Quranic verses treating legal questions (estimated by Ghazali at around five hundred), five hundred hadiths, the abrogated verses, and the reasons and conditions for their abrogation; as well as the knowledge of different cases of consensus and divergence of savants and all the secondary sources in law and jurisprudence; and finally, the exercise of absolute morality and the total mastery of the highest ends of Islamic law? Certainly, of course, there is the idea that whoever engages in interpretation must fit the criteria of competence and intellectual honesty. But fundamentally, ultimately, because the most important thing—the full comprehension of the movement of the world—is subordinated by those scholars to the memory of decisions already made about cases, or simply ignored, we can see how they chain the present to the past. *Ijtihad* becomes the monopoly of an intellectual caste for whom knowledge means recitation.

This is precisely what Iqbal opposes. The stakes of the reconstruction of religious thought in Islam, which is at the heart of his definition of *ijtihad*, are far too important to be left to "technicians." Once again, it is not a matter of technique but of the philosophical reappraisal of a cosmology of emergence, a process undertaken by Iqbal and thought in Bergsonian terms. And nothing, doubtless, would better express the nature of this process than his reflection on time and destiny, the subject of the next chapter.

4

TIME AND FATALISM

Iqbal on Islamic Fatalism

Speaking of the word *destiny*, Muhammad Iqbal writes that it "has been so much misunderstood both in and outside the world of Islam."[1] What Iqbal means is that Muslims themselves have taken the word to mean faith in absolute predestination, while at the same time non-Muslims, identifying Islam with a belief in destiny, have judged it to be a religion based on blind fatalism, stemming from resignation to *maktūb*, or what has been already written. If "a most degrading type of Fatalism has prevailed in the world of Islam for many centuries," he explains, this "was due partly to philosophical thought, partly to political expediency, and partly to the gradually diminishing force of the life-impulse, which Islam originally imparted to its followers."[2] Above all, fatalism is a symptom that signals the exhaustion of élan vital. It is also the case that the Umayyads, whose dynasty was essentially criminally imposed, needed to be able to attribute their abuse to a predestination justifying the fait accompli, which theologians would willingly erect as an article of faith. Finally, Iqbal says, fatalism rests on a philosophy of time and of divine action exercised on the world from the outside in order to make the succession of events into an inevitable chain. It is also in the name of this philosophy that the "European critics of Islam," in Iqbal's words, saw in that religion the very incarnation of belief in destiny. These "European critics" would then include G. W. Leibniz. In his varying responses to the accusation that his system inevitably led to necessitarianism and fatalism, Leibniz consistently emphasized that his concept of necessity must not be conflated with another doctrine, which had to be distinguished from it: Islamic fatalism, for which he created the expressions "*fatum mahometanum*" or "fate after the Turkish [i.e., Islamic] fashion."

In what follows, we will compare Leibniz's assertions about *fatum mahometanum*, or Islamic fatalism, with the manner in which the question of predestination was debated in Islamic theology and philosophy, and with what—in Bergsonian terms—Muhammad Iqbal says about it. With Iqbal, we will contend that ultimately it is only thinking time as duration that permits an escape from the antinomy in which the question of predestination is, in general, inscribed; only thinking time as duration allows truly thinking the amor fati without fatalism that Leibniz intended as the hallmark of his system.

LEIBNIZ ON *FATUM MAHOMETANUM*

In the preface to his *Theodicy*, Leibniz writes:

> There are two famous labyrinths where our reason goes astray: one concerns the great question of the Free and the Necessary, above all in the production and the origin of Evil; the other consists in the discussion of continuity and of the indivisibles which appear to be the elements thereof, and where the consideration of the infinite must enter in. The first perplexes almost all the human race, the other exercises philosophers only.[3]

Because of the practical, not speculative, nature of his enterprise, the thinker of "pre-established harmony"—as he liked to refer to himself—would only explore the first labyrinth: the freedom of man and the justice of God. The end here is to establish a God who is to be "imitated" and "loved" as the sole object of true devotion, a God to whose will we "are resigned to . . . knowing that what he wills is best," and not a "despotic power" corresponding to a "false conception of necessity." This false conception is the belief that "the future [being] necessary, that which must happen will happen, whatever I may do" and therefore results in "lazy reason." Necessity is here associated with (1) divine foreknowledge, which predicts or pre-establishes everything, (2) the determined "concatenation of causes," and (3) the notion that an assertion that a future event will take place could be true or false even though we do not always know which it is.

The phrase "What God wills is best" is thus for Leibniz the key to understanding that divine power is not despotic; instead, it is perfectly compatible with freedom. The freedom of a despot, furthermore, should be labeled "whim,"[4] whereas God exercises true freedom, in his wisdom choosing to bring into existence only the best world out of all the possible worlds his understanding envisions. Consequently, the existing world is not the best because God willed it, but it was willed by him because it was the best of all equally possible worlds with the same right to exist.

Of course, this raises the following questions: Does this mean that the best possible world has imposed its necessity upon God, so to speak? And if that is the case, is it not pure fiction to state that other worlds were ever possible? Could these worlds preserve some possible existence, even if there was never any question of them becoming real? We know that for Spinoza, the notion of a simple possible is meaningless. Leibniz, however, needs a positive concept of the possible in order to maintain God's choice as a true one and also so that his making of this world in accordance with the principle of the best (which is a form of the principle of sufficient reason) does not depend on some "metaphysical," "geometrical," or "absolute" necessity but on "moral" or "hypothetical" necessity. This distinction between metaphysical necessity and moral necessity is crucial for Leibniz's defense of God's justice (theodicy), which is incompatible with absolute necessity.

This is why Leibniz demonstrates some impatience with Samuel Clarke when, in his *Fourth Reply* (June 26, 1716), the British philosopher writes that Leibniz's doctrine "leads to universal necessity and fate, by supposing that motives have the same relation to the will of an intelligent agent, as weights have to a balance."[5] In response, Leibniz wonders whether his interlocutor is actually "willing to listen and to show that he is a lover of truth," suspecting that he may be more interested in "pick[ing] holes in what [he is] saying, without throwing light on anything." Thus in his *Fifth Response*, his last—he died in November, after having written the response in August of 1716—he repeats the importance of the conceptual distinctions he established in the *Theodicy*, "perhaps better and more fully than anyone else." In particular, he emphasizes that "we must . . . distinguish between a necessity, which takes place because the opposite implies a contradiction; (which necessity is called logical, metaphysical, or mathematical); and a necessity which is moral, whereby, a wise being chooses the best, and every mind follows the strongest inclination."[6] All in all, Leibniz's direct argument that freedom "exempt not only from constraint but also from real necessity" does have its place in his philosophy of the divine calculation and bringing-into-existence of the best possible world consists in showing that what makes a choice free is that another choice is *possible*. God indeed chose the world where the succession of events was only compatible with Caesar crossing the Rubicon, even though an infinite number of other worlds—worlds in which, on the contrary, Caesar humbly conformed himself to the Roman tradition—were also possible. From the point of view of Caesar himself, he chose to cross the Rubicon completely freely, because the decision not to cross it was possible, even though all of his motivations (ambition, sense of destiny, etc.) inclined toward this choice. Again and again, Leibniz insists that to predispose or to incline does not mean to necessitate.

But besides this direct argument, which rests on the logical definition of the possible as that whose opposite does not imply contradiction, Leibniz also offers an indirect argument, which consists in presenting what is, according to him, a doctrine of fate that rests upon a false conception of necessity—presenting this in order to make manifest how radically different his philosophy is from that doctrine. This epitome of absolute necessity is what he calls *fatum mahometanum*, or "fate after the Turkish (i.e. Islamic) fashion." In his response to Clarke, Leibniz returns to the distinction established in the *Theodicy* between *fatum mahometanum*, *fatum stoicum*, and *fatum christianum*. Islamic fatalism, he contends, "implies that such-and-such *will happen* even if its cause is avoided, as though it were absolutely necessary." It amounts to mere *unconsciousness* for Leibniz, who cites as an example the fact that "the Turks . . . do not even abandon places infected with plague, owing to their use of [lazy reason]." Next there is the progress represented by the Stoic conception of fate, which leads to *tranquility* and patience that follow from the realization that it is futile to balk at the course of events. Finally, beyond that tranquility is the *contentment* that is linked to the idea of fate as divine Providence, which is the pleasure taken in "a knowledge of the divine perfections" and an understanding that what God has preordained is "not only for the greatest good in general, but also for the greatest particular good of those who love him."[7] The more complete this understanding, the further we move from the "forced patience" of the Stoics toward the Christian amor fati, the certainty that "it is not even possible to wish for anything better than what [God] does."[8] One reason, Leibniz states, why it is necessary to make this distinction is because this "Turkish fatalism" continuously haunts "most men and even Christians," who are always under the threat of falling back into "lazy reason," particularly under circumstances when they want to cheat themselves. For example, we may refuse to adopt the diet we know is best for us because we do not wish to feel constrained: We thus make recourse to the argument that we ought not to try to resist what God has kept in store for us.

At the same time as his thought is thus defined in opposition to what he calls Islamic fatalism, on the one hand, on the other hand, it is also defined against the other extreme, the opposite of *fatum mahometanum*, which is the doctrine of the "Socinians." The particular aspect of Socinianism at which Leibniz takes aim here is the rejection by the followers of Laelius Socinus (d. 1562, Zurich) and his nephew Faustus Socinus (d. 1604, Poland) of an understanding of a divine omniscience that would eliminate the possibility of human free will. If God knew every future event, freedom would be a contradiction; thus, for them, God's omniscience is limited to necessary truths and does not apply to contingent truths (such as what might happen). In Leibniz's words, the "God of the Socinians . . . lives only from day to day" and "does not so much as foresee inconveniences."[9] He adds that the God of the Newtonians (whom he engages in a philosophical quarrel via Clarke) would see things coming but would have prepared nothing, contenting himself with fixing things after they happened, if need be. Between the Turkish/Muslim perdition and the Socinian heresy stands, Leibniz concludes, the true understanding of God's providence, which leads to amor fati.

We will return to the notion of a God who "lives only from day to day," associated by Leibniz with the Socinians. First, however, in opposition to Leibniz's construction of *fatum mahometanum*, we will turn to the question of fate as it is posed throughout the history of theology and philosophy in the Islamic world—and in particular, in the modern period, in the thought of Muhammad Iqbal.

THE QUESTION OF FATALISM IN ISLAMIC THOUGHT AND IN IQBAL'S PHILOSOPHY

In fact, the example Leibniz gives of the Turks refusing to abandon places infected with plague is not without some basis in the Islamic tradition: It is a reference to an actual Islamic tradition but a truncated one. Most likely the philosopher from Hanover was unaware when citing this example that he was actually more or less repeating a *hadith*. That hadith is narrated in slightly different versions, but in any case it tells the story of the second caliph of Islam, Umar, on an expedition in Syria: "On hearing that the plague was raging in a particular town of Syria, Umar decided not to visit that place. In reply to Abu Ubaydah ibn Al-Jarrah, who had objected to his fleeing from a divinely ordained destiny, he said that Abd Al-Rahman ibn Awf had told him that the Holy Prophet had said, 'If plague breaks out in a place, do not enter if you are not already inside it, but if you are, do not leave it.'"

Far from being a manifestation of "Islamic fatalism," Leibniz's example of the plague is thus part of a continuing discussion in Islamic thought about divine pre-establishment and foreknowledge of all things and human free will. In this particular case, the point is that patience in the face of divine Providence should mean staying in place when plague breaks out, in order not to spread the epidemic any farther—and of course not going to a plague-stricken place if warned. What we witness with this example is the way in which a stereotype (that of the Turk being fatalist by fanaticism) becomes a philosophical argument. What, then, do Muslim intellectual elites themselves have to say about fate and necessity in the discussion of these questions, of which the tradition evoked here is an aspect?

First: it must be noted that it is the question of predestination that essentially gave birth to Islamic theology known as "kalām." To the question of whether we are free to act as we do, the Quran supplies a variety of different answers. Since it is possible to find verses that go in either direction, toward free will or toward determinism, the matter must be decided by reflection. The school of theology known as *muʿtazilism* was famously born out of the rationalist view that God's justice could only make sense if humans exercise absolute free will. Opposed to this school were the partisans of predestination, who insisted upon God's omnipotence and omniscience. The question of the true meaning of God's decree and sentences had been endlessly debated before simply becoming—in a period of decadence in Islamic thought—the popular doctrine of "what is already written" (*maktūb*) and the expression of fatalism and irresponsibility.

In the modern era, it was Muhammad Iqbal who revived the philosophical discussion around this question, meaning that he extended it into a reflection on the larger notion of time. Such reflection is needed to tackle the problem of the "labyrinth" of which Leibniz spoke; Iqbal would declare that what would permit an escape from the impasse of God's omniscience-omnipotence versus free will would be full understanding of the true nature of time as expressed, according to him, by the cosmology of the Quran. And this full understanding is offered through the work of Henri Bergson. Indeed, in *The Reconstruction of Religious Thought in Islam*, Iqbal writes: "The truth is that the whole theological controversy relating to predestination is due to pure speculation with no eye on the spontaneity of life, which is a fact of actual experience."[10]

This "the spontaneity of life" is at the heart of Iqbal's thought and bears the mark of the influence of the Bergsonian élan vital. Of course, this influence was possible because of thinking already present in Islamic thought: the vitalism and evolutionary thinking found, for example, in the Sufi poet Jalāl al-Dīn Rūmī, whom Iqbal saw as one of his masters. Here is a passage from Rūmī's *Mathnavī*, famous for the evolutionism it expresses:

First man appeared in the class of inorganic things
Next he passed therefrom into that of plants.
For years he lived as one of the plants,
Remembering naught of his inorganic state so different;
And when he passed from the vegetative to the animal state
He had no remembrance of his state as a plant,
Except the inclination he felt to the world of plants,

> Especially at the time of spring and sweet flowers.
> Like the inclination of infants towards their mothers,
> Which knows not the cause of their inclination to the breast . . .
> Again the great Creator, as you know,
> Drew man out of the animal into the human state.
> Thus man passed from one order of nature to another,
> Till he became wise and knowing and strong as he is now.
> Of his first souls he has now no remembrance.
> And he will be again changed from his present soul.[11]

Ultimately, fatalism rests upon a cosmology of a closed world in which the future is determined—kept in store, so to speak, and ready to be deployed according to a fixed and necessary order of events that appears to limit even God's action. This is Newton's universe, which Iqbal describes as "a collection of finite things, [which] presents itself as a kind of island situated in a pure vacuity to which time, regarded as a series of mutually exclusive moments, is nothing and does nothing."[12]

What does it mean that in such a cosmology time is said to be nothing and to do nothing? To answer that question is to understand the importance of the revolution represented by Bergson in the history of philosophy, and in particular in the thinking of time, as evoked in our discussion of what Senghor called "the 1889 revolution." Against a philosophical tradition in which what is in the process of becoming can never be apprehended by reason, Bergson contends that to know is not always to immobilize, to fix, to hold beneath the gaze; it can also be to enter the flow of things, to "dance" the object, to return to Senghor's words. No longer is time fixed, as "a number belonging to change with respect to the before and after,"[13] which is itself only a composition, a juxtaposition of immobilities. As Bergson writes, this manner of thinking things "cannot deal with time and motion except on condition of first eliminating the essential and qualitative element—of time, duration, and motion, mobility."[14] We can easily understand this, Bergson continues, "by examining the part played in astronomy and mechanics by considerations of time, motion, and velocity."[15]

In short: our analytic intelligence constructs spatialized time, time reduced simply to being an "interval." For Bergson, the cause of this state of things is the cinematographic method that has been imposed on our modern science, just as it was imposed on the ancients.

Now we can understand what Iqbal meant: The time that is nothing and does nothing is the serial time that is reduced to the distance separating different events on a trajectory between the present and the past that could just as well extend into the future. This time, Iqbal says, is "deprive[d] of its living historical character and reduce[d] . . . to a mere representation of space."[16] As

Bergson says, this is the time of astronomy and mechanics; it is also the time of astrology and foresight. If time occurs as a trajectory, a geometrical line or frame that can always be extended or expanded, effectively there is room for a possible point of view—that of a God or an astrologer—for which future events would present themselves as foreknown. More precisely, in fact there would be no *event*, strictly speaking. Past and future would both stretch out before an all-encompassing vision, such as that of the intelligence according to Laplace, that would see the end in the beginning. Opposed to this is the time we can intuit as duration, even if we speak of it in a language made for serial time. This time is not a frame within which events are disposed *partes extra partes*. On the contrary, events are the unfolding of duration—or, to use a Bergsonian metaphor, its snowballing with itself. As Iqbal writes:

> Most of our theologians thought the doctrine of human freedom could not be reconciled with the foreknowledge of God. They looked upon belief in freedom as veiled atheism. So thought Mahmud Shabistari (a Sufi who died in 1317). But the author of *The Secret Rose Garden* . . . made the tacit assumption of an absolute and independent Time like Newton. He did not see that if his view of Time were true, then the freedom of God would also disappear. Shabistari's argument will not hold today; for God can be conceived as creating Time from moment to moment. If

> the Universe is an open one, there is no pre-existing future, and God does not know the future because there is nothing to know.[17]

There is nothing to know because what would be here to know is that "everything" that Bergson had shown was only a pseudo-idea, the use of which had led to "false problems": "What exactly does 'omnipotence' mean?" asks Bergson in *The Two Sources of Morality and Religion*, which explains:

> We have shown that the idea of "nothing" is tantamount to the idea of a square circle, that it vanished under analysis, only leaving an empty word behind it, in fine that it is a pseudo-idea. May not the same apply to the idea of "everything," if this name is given not only to the sum-total of the real, but also to the totality of the possible? I can, at a stretch, represent something in my mind when I hear of the sum total of existing things, but in the sum-total of the non-existent I can see nothing but a string of words.[18]

An understanding of the cosmology of the Quran as "creative evolution," rather than as a creation once and for all completed, an "everything": According to Iqbal, this is the substance of the Bergsonian "revolution." Such an understanding would newly reveal the meaning of certain verses, some cited earlier: "He adds to His creation what He wills" (35:1) or "See they not how God bringeth forth creation? and then causeth it to return again? This truly is easy for God. Say, go through the earth, and see how he hath brought forth created beings. Hereafter, with a second birth will God cause them to be born again; for God is Almighty" (29:19–20) or "Everyday doth some new work employ Him" (55:29). In addition to these, we can repeat the prophetic saying Iqbal often cited: "Do not vilify time, for time is God."

As for the *fatum*, which correlates to the cinematographic conception of time, Iqbal uses the Arabic word *qismat* for it, explaining that this means the "lot" or "share" that falls to each person. This corresponds to the notion that each individual has a share laid up for them in the future, which is gradually delivered according to a predetermined order of events. It is such a conception of time—even more than the notion of fate—that Leibniz characterized as "Turkish" or "Islamic," and as an attitude of passive resignation before an external divine will. But for Iqbal, this is a perversion of what he designates, using another Arabic word, as *taqdir*, or what he characterizes as an "active fatalism." *Qdr*, of which *taqdir* is a derivative, signifies power. If this word is translated as *destiny*, it is in the sense of he who carries it with him, and it is linked to the conception of time that Iqbal calls "pure time":

> Pure time . . . as revealed by a deeper analysis of our conscious experience, is not a string of separate, reversible instants; it is an organic whole in which the

> past is not left behind, but is moving along with, and operating in, the present. And the future is given to it not as lying before, yet to be traversed; it is given only in the sense that it is present in its nature as an open possibility. It is time regarded as an organic whole that the Quran describes as *taqdir* or the destiny—a word which has been so much misunderstood both in and outside the world of Islam.[19]

Following Iqbal, we can now speak of destiny in the sense in which we can speak of belief in one's destiny as one's capacity to shape the course of events. Iqbal's active fatalism is the fatalism of people of action; it is Caesar declaring "alea jacta est" as he crossed the Rubicon, or Napoleon exclaiming, "I am a thing, not a person," or Muawiya, the founder of the Umayyad dynasty, who proclaimed, "I am destiny," or his opponent the fourth caliph, Ali, who for his part uttered, "I am the living Quran." At the moment of these declarations, each of these "great men" saw himself from the outside, as it were, as the instrument of history as it was being written. They felt themselves full of the possibilities carried by time.

In his poetry, which he considered to be more philosophical than philosophy, Iqbal expresses this active fatalism through a multiplicity of images. In *Gabriel's Wing*, for example, he writes:

> What do astrologers know about thy fate?
> Living dust thou art, not a slave of stars.[20]

Or, from the same collection of poems:

> Raise thy selfhood so high that before each dis-
> pensation
> God Himself may ask thee what thy wishes are.[21]

To conclude, let us return to the God of the Socinians, who "lives only from day to day." As we have seen, Leibniz denounces a God who would be limited in his knowledge of future events as contradictory. On this point he is correct. The Socinians, however, rightly maintain that a God who knows all predetermined events completely contradicts all idea of freedom, God's and that of the creatures he creates in his image. Behind both ways of asking the question and perceiving the contradiction lies the same Eleatic notion of a spatialized time in which an "everything" is inscribed. Leibniz's philosophy is no stranger to vitalism or to evolutionary thinking, as we know. But his thinking of time, especially with respect to his description of *fatum mahometanum*, tends more toward his mechanistic Cartesian outlook than his philosophical vitalism; he continues to understand time through analogies with space. In the folding of the one upon the other, time is still kept apart from its dynamism, and thus the questions of fate and necessity come to seem an inescapable labyrinth. In fact, only the Bergsonian revolution would permit a single step outside the bounds of serial time and allow *fatum mahometanum* to manifest its true, active meaning.

CONCLUSION

As a brief conclusion, we will interrogate the Bergsonism that Senghor and Iqbal each shaped for the purposes of their respective thought. In the case of Senghor, even if he constantly evoked the "1889 revolution" (and thus *Time and Free Will*), his Bergson was above all the Bergson of *Creative Evolution*. In the philosophy of life that this work contains, first, Senghor found something that he wanted to connect to the notion of vital force, which he had seen as the heart of the ontology of indigenous African religions, and the thought that these inspired, from his very first writings onward. Above all, he needed support for his thesis of an approach to the real that differed from the rational way—the approach that was, he claimed, revealed through African art. The Bergson in which Senghor was most interested was the Bergson who dissociated modes of knowledge: the Bergson who, as Frédéric Worms wrote, "*brought us back* from the intellect, as a *partial* result *opposed to others*, to a *primitive unity* of life."[1] Senghor's Bergson was the Bergson of vital understanding who emphasized that "the intellect is characterized by a natural inability to comprehend life."[2]

As for Muhammad Iqbal's Bergsonism, we might go back to the word "affinity" that Massignon used to describe Iqbal's relationship to Bergson's philosophy. What this word tells us is that, rather than "applying" Bergson's concepts, Iqbal truly thought *with* him. It is therefore remarkable that, at many points, his *Reconstruction of Religious Thought in Islam* echoes the French philosopher's writings in *The Two Sources of Morality and Religion*. This is all the more remarkable considering the fact that, as we know, Iqbal gave the lectures brought together in this work between 1928 and 1930, while Bergson's book was published in 1932.

Is this because the substance of *The Two Sources* was already contained in Bergson's previous works, to which Iqbal had access and that he cited? We could indeed make this argument, although Brigitte Sitbon-Peillon has shown that Bergson's "method" was precisely not a "system" where, from a set of principles, different applications to religion, or to mysticism, for example, could be necessarily derived.[3] We should also note that, like Bergson in *The Two Sources*, Iqbal constructed his thought on the idea that at the beginning is the religious *experience* of the mystics: The "proof" of God's existence depends on the lived experience of it by the mystics.[4]

Iqbal's philosophy of becoming-individual rested not on the notion of contemplation but on a "complete mysticism," the action of the one who achieves ascension only in and for the task of "complet[ing] the creation of the human species"[5]: the one whose "direction is the same as *élan vital*" and creates an "open society." In the case of Bergson and Iqbal—above and beyond "influence"—it is right to speak of an "affinity."

ACKNOWLEDGMENTS

I thank Henry Laurens, who invited me to deliver the lectures that have become this book at the Collège de France from December 18, 2009, to January 18, 2010. I am grateful to those who attended the lectures and made useful comments. Some of those comments have found their way into the book. Thank you also to the colleagues and friends with whom I have discussed Bergson, Senghor, and Iqbal for many years: I mention especially, in no particular order, Brent Hayes, Gary Wilder, Mamadou Diouf, Frédéric Worms, Nadia Yala Kisukidi, Bado Ndoye, Hady Ba, Oumar Dia, Babacar Mbaye Diop, Ramatoulaye Diagne-Mbengue, Nasrin Qader, Donna Jones, Vincent Debaene, and Françoise Blum. I also thank my students whose comments during our discussions contributed to the book; among them, I mention Mounia Abousaid, *in memoriam*.

NOTES

FOREWORD: LOCATING THE POSTCOLONIAL IDEA

1. Souleymane Bachir Diagne, *The Ink of the Scholars*, trans. Jonathan Adjemian (Dakar: CODESRIA, 2016), 1–2.

2. See Césaire's important essay "Culture and Colonization," trans. Brent Hayes Edwards, *Social Text* 28, no. 2 (103) (2010): 127–44.

3. Léopold Senghor, "Education," in *Senghor: Prose & Poetry*, ed. and trans. John Reed and Clive Wake (London: Oxford University Press, 1965), 53.

4. Senghor, "Education," 53–54.

5. Léopold Senghor, "Cultural Roots and the Modern African Artist," in *Senghor: Prose & Poetry*, ed. and trans. John Reed and Clive Wake (London: Oxford University Press, 1965), 76.

6. Léopold Senghor, "Towards a New African-Inspired Humanism," in *Senghor: Prose & Poetry*, ed. and trans. John Reed and Clive Wake (London: Oxford University Press, 1965), 78.

7. Léopold Senghor, "Association and Assimilation," in *Senghor: Prose & Poetry*, ed. and trans. John Reed and Clive Wake (London: Oxford University Press, 1965), 52.

8. This comment is reproduced in Léopold Senghor, "We Are All Cultural Half-Castes," in *Senghor: Prose and Poetry*, ed. and trans. John Reed and Clive Wake (London: Oxford University Press, 1965), 75.

9. Senghor, "Education," 54.

10. Souleymane Bachir Diagne, "Toward an Intellectual History of West Africa: The Meaning of Timbuktu," in *The Meanings of Timbuktu*, ed. Shamil Jeppie and Souleymane Bachir Diagne (Cape Town: HSRC Press, 2008), 26.

INTRODUCTION

1. *Annales Bergsoniennes*, vol. 5, *Bergson et la Politique: de Jaurès à Aujourd'hui*, ed. Frédéric Worms (Paris: PUF, 2012).

2. Henri Bergson, "Discours en séance publique de l'Academie des sciences morales et politiques," in *Melanges* (Paris: Presses universitaires de France, 1972), 1107. Bergson's speech was published in English in 1915 under the title *The Meaning of War: Life and Matter in*

Conflict, trans. H. Wildon-Carr (London: T. Fisher Unwin). Unfortunately, the first paragraph from which the quote is made was not translated.

3. For more about the journal, see Adel A. Ziadat, *Western Science in the Arab World: The Impact of Darwinism, 1860–1930* (New York: Palgrave McMillan, 1986), and Marwa Elshakry, *Reading Darwin in Arabic, 1860–1950* (Chicago: University of Chicago Press, 2013).

4. Elshakry, *Reading Darwin in Arabic*, 4.

5. Elshakry, 26.

6. Elshakry, 128.

7. Henri Bergson, *Mind-Energy: Lectures and Essays*, trans. H. Wildon Carr (Westport, Conn.: Greenwood Press, 1975), 27–29.

8. Bergson, *Mind-Energy*, 31–32.

9. Damian A. Howard, *Being Human in Islam: The Impact of the Evolutionary Worldview* (New York: Routledge, 2011), 51–52.

10. Howard, *Being Human in Islam*, 187n190.

11. Howard, 79.

12. Howard, 57.

13. Howard (187n190) cites H. Goddard's *A History of Christian-Muslim Relations* (Edinburgh: Edinburgh University Press, 2000).

14. "Souleymane Bachir Diagne represents the latest wave of Bergsonian Islam," he writes. Howard, *Being Human in Islam*, 84.

15. Souleymane Bachir Diagne, *Islam et société ouverte, la fidélité et le mouvement dans la pensée de*

Muhammad Iqbal (Paris: Maisonneuve & Larose, 2001).

16. Souleymane Bachir Diagne, *Islam and Open Society: Fidelity and Movement in the Philosophy of Muhammad Iqbal*, trans. Melissa McMahon (Dakar: CODESRIA, 2011).

17. Souleymane Bachir Diagne, *Léopold Sédar Senghor, l'art africain comme philsophie* (Paris: Riveneuve Editions, 2007).

18. Souleymane Bachir Diagne, *African Art as Philosophy: Senghor, Bergson, and the Idea of Negritude*, trans. Chike Jeffers (New York: Seagull Books, 2011).

19. Muhammad Iqbal, *The Secrets of the Self*, trans. R. A. Nicholson, rev. ed. (Karachi, Pakistan: Oxford University Press, 2004), lines 1571–72 and 1575–79.

20. Iqbal, *Secrets of the Self*, lines 947–53.

21. Frédéric Worms, *Bergson ou les deux sens de la vie* (Paris: PUF, 2004), 8.

22. A solicitation from the journal *Qui Parle* let me take up Bergson, Iqbal, and Senghor in an article entitled "Bergson in the Colony," later translated and published in French in the issue of *Annales bergsoniennes* (vol. 5) mentioned earlier.

23. In "The Soul and the Body," a lecture delivered at "Foi et Vie" on April 28, 1912. In Bergson, *Mind-Energy*, 57.

24. Bergson speaks of "the creation of self by self, the growing of the personality by an effort which draws much from little, something from nothing, and

adds unceasingly to whatever wealth the world contains." Bergson, *Mind-Energy*, 30–31.

25. The Bandung Conference, an Afro-Asian meeting that took place in 1955 to condemn European colonialism, can be considered the beginning of the postcolonial era.

1. BERGSONISM IN THE THOUGHT OF LÉOPOLD SÉDAR SENGHOR

1. Léopold Sédar Senghor, *Liberté V: Le dialogue des cultures* (Paris: Seuil, 1993), 192–98.

2. Frédéric Worms speaks of the "philosophical moment of 1900," explaining that "if we distinguish a philosophical 'moment' by both the presence of characteristics external to the works themselves—above all by *the state of knowledge and a major controversy* that breaks with what came before it, and the presence of characteristics internal to the works, above all *common problems and singular positions* which truly constitute its novelty—we can immediately see that Bergson at once occupies a place at the heart of what will become, thanks to his thought, the '1900 moment' in philosophy." Frédéric Worms, *Bergson ou les deux sens de la vie* (Paris: PUF, 2004), 21.

3. Henri Bergson, *Time and Free Will: An Essay on the Immediate Data of Consciousness*, trans. F. L. Pogson (London: George Allen, 1913 [repr.; Dover, 2001]), 225.

4. Bergson, *Time and Free Will*, 230.

5. Bergson, 144.

6. See Alain Berthoz and Jean-Luc Petit, *The Physiology and Phenomenology of Action*, trans. Christopher Macann (Oxford: Oxford University Press, 2008).

7. Stanislas Adotévi, *Négritude et Négrologues* (Paris: le Code Astral, 1998), 49–50.

8. Léopold Sédar Senghor, *Liberté 1: Négritude et Humanisme* (Paris: Seuil, 1964), 43.

9. Senghor, *Liberté 1*, 168.

10. Henri Bergson, *The Two Sources of Morality and Religion*, trans. R. Ashley Audra and Cloudesley Brereton (London: McMillan, 1935), 119–20.

11. Bergson, *Two Sources of Morality and Religion*, 120–21.

12. Bergson, 121.

13. Bergson, 121.

14. This is recorded by Pierre-Maxime Schuhl, in "Homage to Lévy-Bruhl," *Revue philosophique de la France et de l'Étranger* 4 (October–December 1957): 399.

15. Emmanuel Lévinas, *Entre Nous: Thinking-of-the-Other*, trans. Michael B. Smith and Barbara Harshav (New York: Continuum, 2008), 35.

16. Benoît de l'Estoile, *Le goût des Autres: De l'Exposition coloniale aux Arts premiers* (Paris: Flammarion, 2007). De l'Estoile cites Mauss: "Colonial and French youth could now experience these 'beauties'" (68).

17. Senghor made this declaration in "Le dialogue des cultures," a 1983 lecture at the University of Tübingen (reproduced in *Liberté V. Le dialogue des cultures*, 208).

2. SENGHOR'S AFRICAN SOCIALISM

1. Nigerian writer Wole Soyinka sees Senghor as a model for those Africans who, he says, lay down "the burden of memory" in order to embrace "the muse of forgiveness." Today, he writes, we can find in Senghor the poetic anticipation of what would be the South African Truth and Reconciliation Commission (*The Burden of Memory, the Muse of Forgiveness* [Oxford: Oxford University Press, 1999]).

2. In a report to the inaugural congress of the Parti de la Fédération Africaine, held in Dakar on July 1, 1959, he declared: "What unites us is a common resolve to build step by step a federal State, better still, a Negro-African nation, freely associated with France in a confederation." (Léopold Sédar Senghor, "Nationhood: Report on the Doctrine and Program of the Party of African Federation," in *On African Socialism*, trans. Mercer Cook [New York: Frederick A. Praeger, 1964], 7). For more on this question of a Franco-African confederation, which at one point represented the vision Senghor opposed to the Balkanization of Africa, see Gary Wilder's excellent book, *The French Imperial Nation-State: Negritude and Colonial Humanism*

between the Two World Wars (Chicago: University of Chicago Press, 2005).

3. Janet G. Vaillant, *Black, French, and African: A Life of Léopold Sédar Senghor* (Cambridge, Mass.: Harvard University Press, 1990).

4. Soyinka, *Burden of Memory*.

5. [Translator's note: The French word Césaire uses for Senghor, in the slang of French university students at the time, is *talla*, from "ils von**t-à-la messe**," or "they go to mass."]

6. The very selective agrégation test made successful candidates high-ranked teachers.

7. Jacqueline Sorel, *Léopold Sédar Senghor, l'émotion et la raison* (Paris: Sépia, 1995).

8. These socialist classmates often wrote for *L'Université républicaine*, the publication associated with the league. In the first issue (April 1, 1930), for example, we find an article by Senghor's friend Georges Pompidou against L'action française.

9. Senghor thus belongs to the category of those denounced by Émile Bottigelli in his "Presentation" of the *Manuscripts* he translated into French (this is dated January 15, 1962). He deems those who "see in the *Manuscripts* a fundamentally ethical thought" "social democrats." They would "read the manuscripts as Marx giving philosophical form to his indignation regarding the human condition under the capitalist regime. This revolt would in turn be the real basis of this thought, the later works doing nothing more

than more or less faithfully translating this moral ideal in the language of economy or politics." This interpretation, which he opposes to the "revolutionary" one of Marxist-Leninism, is certainly in line with Senghor's.

10. Léopold Sédar Senghor, *Liberté II, Nation et voie africaine du socialism* (Paris: Seuil, 1971), 31.

11. Karl Marx, "Alienated Labor," in *Marx's Concept of Man*, by Erich Fromm, trans. T. B. Bottomore (New York: Continuum, 2003), 80.

12. Mamadou Dia, *Islam, Societies Africaines et Culture Industrielle* (Dakar: Les Nouvelles Éditions Africaines, 1975), 64, emphasis added.

13. Léopold Sédar Senghor, *Liberté III, Négritude et civilization de l'universel* (Paris: Seuil, 1977), 245.

14. Aimé Césaire, "Letter to Maurice Thorez," trans. Chike Jeffers, *Social Text* 28, no. 2 (103) (summer 2010): 145–52. Maurice Thorez was then the secretary general of the French Communist Party.

15. It is worth noting that recently, the third president of Senegal had a monument seemingly proclaiming the glory of Soviet realism in art erected on the highest point in Dakar—despite strong opposition to the project motivated by religious, economic, and, above all, aesthetic reasons—and by a North Korean company, no less.

16. Léopold Sédar Senghor, *On African Socialism*, trans. Mercer Cook (New York: Frederick A. Praeger, 1964).

17. Senghor, *On African Socialism*, 20–21. September 28, 1958, is the date of the referendum proposed to African populations, who had to decide whether to stay within the frame of the "*Communauté*" with France or to take their independence immediately, as Guinea did. Italics in the text are Senghor's.

18. Senghor, 21–22.

19. Senghor, 5. [Translator's note: The last word is in English in the original.]

20. Speaking of the creation by France of the French West African Federation, Senghor writes: "France borrowed, for her own use, the great design of the emperors of Mali and Songhai: to link Senegal to the Hausa country, the Sahara oases to the Gulf of Benin, in order to group the 'Sudanese' races into a politically and economically viable entity. Why should what was good for France and Black Africa in the first half of the twentieth century no longer be so in the second half?" (Senghor, 15). The author contrasts France's attitude and England's, which wanted to keep the Nigerian Federation intact after independence despite centrifugal forces (19).

21. Senghor, 5–6.

22. G. W. F. Hegel, *Philosophy of Right*, trans. S. W. Dyde (Kitchener, Ontario: Batoche Books, 2001), 14.

23. Senghor, 32. "One people, one goal, one faith" was the motto chosen by Senegal on its own after the breakup of the short-lived Mali Federation.

24. Gaston Berger, *Shaping the Future: Gaston Berger and the Concept of Prospective*, ed. André Cournand and Maurice Lévy (New York: Gordon and Breach Science Publishers, 1973), 27.

25. Berger, *Shaping the Future*, 29.

26. Mamadou Dia and the team he created around the Dominican Father Louis-Joseph Lebret would put this vision of planning to work.

3. BERGSON, IQBAL, AND THE CONCEPT OF *IJTIHAD*

1. Louis Massignon, preface to *Reconstruire la pensée religieuse de l'islam*, by Muhammad Iqbal, trans. Éva Meyerovitch (Paris: Librairie d'Amérique et d'Orient Adrien-Maisonneuve, 1955), 3.

2. Nikki R. Keddie, *An Islamic Response to Imperialism: Political and Religious Writings of Sayyid Jamâl ad-Dîn 'al-Afghânî* (Berkeley: University of California Press, 1983), 122.

3. Muhammad Iqbal, *Stray Reflections: The Private Notebook of Muhammad Iqbal* (Lahore: Iqbal Academy Pakistan, 2008), 112.

4. Muhammad Iqbal, "Presidential Address," in *Speeches, Writings, and Statements of Iqbal*, ed. Latif Ahmed Sherwani, 2nd ed., 3–26 (1944; repr. Lahore: Iqbal Academy, 1977). Drawn from text edited here: http://www.columbia.edu/itc/mealac/pritchett/00islamlinks/txt_iqbal_1930.html.

5. Iqbal, "Presidential Address."

6. Iqbal, "Presidential Address."
7. Iqbal, "Presidential Address."
8. Iqbal, "Presidential Address."
9. Iqbal, "Presidential Address."
10. Iqbal, "Presidential Address."
11. Iqbal, "Presidential Address."
12. Iqbal, "Presidential Address."
13. G. W. Leibniz, *Philosophical Essays*, trans. and ed. Roger Ariew and Dan Garber (Indianapolis: Hackett, 1989), 86.
14. "Vital properties are never entirely realized, though always on the way to become so; they are no so much *states* as *tendencies*. . . . In particular, it may be said of individuality that, while the tendency to individuate is everywhere present in the organized world, it is everywhere opposed by the tendency towards reproduction." Henri Bergson, *Key Writings*, ed. Keith Ansell Pearson and John Ó Maoilearca (London: Continuum, 2002), 178.

4. TIME AND FATALISM: IQBAL ON ISLAMIC FATALISM

1. Muhammad Iqbal, *The Reconstruction of Religious Thought in Islam*, intro. by Javed Majeed (Stanford, Calif.: Stanford University Press, 2013), 40.
2. Iqbal, *Reconstruction of Religious Thought in Islam*, 88.
3. G. W. Leibniz, *Theodicy: Essays on the Goodness of God, the Freedom of Man, and the Origin of Evil*, ed.

Austin Farrer, trans. E. M. Huggard (La Salle, Ill.: Open Court, 1985), 53.

4. In his *Fourth Reply* (June 2, 1716), in response to the *Third Reply* by Clarke, Leibniz writes that "a mere will without any motive, is a fiction, not only contrary to God's perfection, but also chimerical and contradictory; inconsistent with the definition of the will, and sufficiently confuted in my *Theodicy*." H. G. Alexander, ed., *The Leibniz-Clarke Correspondence* (New York: Manchester University Press, 1956), 36.

5. Alexander, *Leibniz-Clarke Correspondence*, 45.

6. Alexander, 56.

7. Alexander, 58.

8. Alexander, 55.

9. Alexander, 19.

10. Iqbal, *Reconstruction of Religious Thought in Islam*, 63.

11. Quoted in Iqbal, *Reconstruction of Religious Thought in Islam*, 97. Two things stand out about this passage quoted by Iqbal. The first is its Teilhardian overtones: Iqbal's French translator, Éva Meyerovitch, indicates that Iqbal and Pierre Teilhard de Chardin were acquainted (*Islam, l'autre visage* [Paris: Albin Michel, 1991], 37). We might surmise that they shared the same feeling of affinity that Massignon described between Iqbal and Bergson. Senghor was not wrong when he spoke of Iqbal as a "Muslim Teilhard." The second is that Leibniz's thought contains a comparable evolutionary strain.

12. Iqbal, *Reconstruction of Religious Thought in Islam*, 105.

13. Aristotle, *Physics* (219b), trans. C. D. C. Reeve (Indianapolis: Hackett, 2018), 77.

14. Henri Bergson, *Key Writings*, ed. Keith Ansell Pearson and John Ó Maoilearca (London: Continuum, 2002), 66.

15. Bergson, *Key Writings*, 66.

16. Iqbal, *Reconstruction of Religious Thought in Islam*, 106.

17. Muhammad Iqbal, *Stray Reflections: The Private Notebook of Muhammad Iqbal* (Lahore: Iqbal Academy Pakistan, 2008), 159.

18. Henri Bergson, *The Two Sources of Morality and Religion*, trans. R. Ashley Audra and Cloudesley Brereton (London: McMillan, 1935), 224–25.

19. Iqbal, *Reconstruction of Religious Thought in Islam*, 39–40. Iqbal summarizes Bergson's thought: "Reality is a free unpredictable, creative vital impetus of the nature of volition which thought spatializes and views as a plurality of 'things'" (41).

20. *Gabriel's Wing*, like other poetry by Iqbal, is available on the site http://www.allamaiqbal.com/. *Gabriel's Wing* (http://www.allamaiqbal.com/poetry.php?bookbup=24&lang_code=en&lang=2) is composed of numbered poems. These verses are found in poem 21, in the English translation of Akbar Ali Shah. The title of the poem is its first line: "Selfhood Is an Ocean Boundless, Fathomless."

21. Iqbal, *Gabriel's Wing*, poem 33, trans. K. A. Shafique. The title of the poem is "Why Should I Ask the Sages about My Origin?"

CONCLUSION

1. Frédéric Worms, *Bergson ou les deux sens de la vie* (Paris: PUF, 2004), 222.

2. Henri Bergson, *Creative Evolution*, trans. Arthur Mitchell (Minneola, N.Y.: Dover, 1998), 165. Worms explains this point, recalling what misunderstandings it might engender. As we have seen, Senghor himself—with his unfortunate phrase opposing reason and emotion—did not escape this type of misunderstanding.

3. Brigitte Sitbon-Peillon, *Religion, Métaphysique, et Sociologies Chez Bergson: Une Expérience Intégral* (Paris: PUF, 2009). See Sitbon-Peillon's introduction for the confusion between "system" and "method" and its consequences.

4. Sitbon-Peillon, *Religion, Métaphysique, et Sociologies Chez Bergson*, 16. [Translator's note: The French word for "proof," *preuve*, is contained within the word used in the original for "ordeal," *épreuve*.]

5. Henri Bergson, *The Two Sources of Morality and Religion*, trans. R. Ashley Audra and Cloudesley Brereton (London: McMillan, 1935), 200.

INDEX

Souleymane Bachir Diagne is Professor of Philosophy and Francophone Studies at Columbia University. His most recent publications are *The Ink of the Scholars: Reflections on Philosophy in Africa* (CODESRIA, 2016) and *Open to Reason: Muslim Philosophers in Conversation with the Western Tradition* (Columbia University Press, 2018).

Lindsay Turner is a poet and translator. She is an assistant professor in the Department of English and Literary Arts at the University of Denver.

John E. Drabinski is Charles Hamilton Houston 1915 Professor of Black Studies at Amherst College.

Milton Keynes UK
Ingram Content Group UK Ltd.
UKHW010337180724
445696UK00004B/130